Flies of the Northwest

Inland Empire Fly Fishing Club

Flies of the Northwest

Inland Empire Fly Fishing Club

Editor-in-Chief: Randy Shaber
Artist: Gene Lorenson
Writer-Editors: Fenton Roskelley   Don Chinn   Bob Bates
Final Editors: Tom Chapman   Richard Ripley
Contributing Writers: Walt Balek   Les Johnson
Photographer: Jim Schollmeyer
Committee Members:
Dry Fly: Dick O'Dell, Tony Roche, Byron Johnson, Boyd Matson, Bob Glaza, Greg Bever, George Potter, Fred Shiosaki, Ray Kranches, Triston Burton, John Propp and Gary Clarke
Wet Fly: Felix Martinez, Clay Findlay, Dave Holmes, Don Chinn, Del Coppock, Dave Gunderson, Jerry Harms, Mike Hart, John Jones, Hubert Langenhorst, Jerry McBride, Jan Sadlo
Steelhead/Salmon: Walt Balek, Gordon Olson, Randy Shaber, Jim Gaddy, Bruce Morgan, Loyd Bibbee, and Pat Whitehill

Acknowledgments

We recognize and thank certain fly anglers, fly tiers, biologists and others who, although likely credited elsewhere in this book have generously shared their time, knowledge, and skills in contributing flies and data for the preparation of this book.

Bob Aid, Kaufmann's, Belleview, Wash.
G.L. Britton and Jim Prudente, Silver Bow Fly Shop, Spokane, Wash.
Tom Darling, Seattle, Wash.
Bruce Ferguson, Tacoma, Wash.
Arnie Gidlow, Missouri Riverside Outfitters and Lodge, Cascade, Mont.
Rick Hafele, Portland, Ore.
René Harrop, House of Harrop, Saint Anthony, Ida.
Dec Hogan, Mt. Vernon, Wash.
Alec Jackson, Kenmore, Wash.
Les Johnson, Seattle, Wash.
Hardy Kruse, The Sport Cove, Spokane, Wash.
Mike Lawson, Henry's Fork Anglers, Last Chance, Ida.
Harry Lemire, Black Diamond, Wash.
Bill Matthews, Gamakatsu USA, Inc., Tacoma, Wash.
Harry Mayo, West Yellowstone, Mont.
Arthur "Mitch" Mikulak, Calgary, Alberta, Canada
Skip Mortensen and John DeVries, O. Mustad and Son (U.S.A.) Inc., Auburn, N.Y.
John Perry, John Perry's Montana Fly Fishing, Missoula, Mont.
John Propp, Propp's Rod and Fly Shop, Spokane, Wash.
Joe Roope, Castaway Fly Fishing Shop, Coeur d'Alene, Ida.
Dave Ruetz, West Bend, Wisc.
John Shewey, Hermiston, Ore.
Rick Smith, Montana's Master Angler, Livingston, Mont.
Chuck Stranahan, Riverbend Fly Shop, Hamilton, Mont.
Tim Tollett, Frontier Anglers, Dillon, Mont.
Jim Toth and others, Grizzly Hackle, Missoula, Mont.
Ken McKnight, Spokane, Wash.

All inquiries should be addressed to:

Frank Amato Publications, Inc.

P.O. Box 82112, Portland, Oregon 97282, 503•653•8108

Book Design: Kathy Johnson
Artwork: Gene Lorenson
Fly Photography: Jim Schollmeyer • Artwork Photography: Randy Shaber
Printed in Canada
Originally published by Inland Empire Fly Fishing Club
Second Edition (Frank Amato Publications, Inc.)
3 5 7 9 10 8 6 4 2

ISBN: 1-57188-065-8
UPC : 0-66066-00315-7

Table of Contents

Preface

*T*his edition of *Flies of the Northwest* is a testament to the wealth of talent, expertise, and devotion in the Inland Empire Fly Fishing Club. As project chairman, I would like to thank personally all of the members and friends of our club who donated their time to prepare this book.

In particular, special thanks is given to the following individuals who worked countless hours on this project:

Our artist, an avid fly fisherman who through his beautiful watercolor paintings captures the essence of fly fishing in the Northwest;

The committee members and their chairmen who sorted through hundreds of fly patterns and selected the most innovative and productive;

The writer-editors who made the final selection of flies and provided most of the text and recipes for the patterns;

The final editors who polished the writings into a more cohesive product;

Our photographer who eloquently displays each of the flies on film;

And finally to Frank Amato and his staff for extending us the compliment of publishing this book.

The text for each chapter in this book was produced by the following lead writers:

Fenton Roskelley: Introduction, A Northwest Fly Fisher's Year, Mayflies, and Chironomids.

Bob Bates: How to use this Book, Caddisflies, Damselflies and Dragonflies, Safety and Etiquette, Catch and Release, Hooks and Caddisfly Hatch Chart.

Don Chinn: Damselflies and Dragonflies: Aquatic Bugs, Aquatic Worms, Leeches, Attractor, Multipurpose, and Miscellaneous Patterns, Fly-fishing for Shad.

Randy Shaber: Stoneflies, Terrestrials, the Land-dwelling Insects, Crustaceans, the Hard-shelled Invertebrates, and Streamers.

Walt Balek: Flies and Fly-fishing for Steelhead, Saltwater and Freshwater Fly-fishing for Salmon, Fly-fishing for Sea-run Cutthroat.

Les Johnson: Saltwater Fly-fishing.

My sincere apologies to anyone inadvertently not credited here for their efforts in preparing this book. Also, please note that considerable effort was made to credit the originator of each fly listed in this book. Any errors or omissions regarding originators are unintentional.

Randy Shaber
Spokane, Washington

Introduction

The Inland Empire Fly Fishing Club is proud to present this sixth edition of *Flies of the Northwest.* It is the culmination of 30 years of publishing information on patterns of special interest to fly fishers who fish Northwest waters.

The club, organized in 1956, produced its first mimeographed patterns booklet, with line drawings, in 1962. Continued revisions have updated the information and patterns.

Any fly fisher, beginner or expert, can use the information in this book to catch trout, steelhead, salmon, sea-run cutthroat, and even shad.

These fly patterns have proven effective at Northwest lakes and streams. Articles and watercolors in this book depict life cycles of insects that trout eat, how the insects behave during various stages of their lives, what patterns fishermen should use to imitate the insects, and how to fish these patterns. The book also includes articles on fly-fishing for steelhead, salmon and sea-run cutthroat. In short, *Flies of the Northwest* is more than a fly pattern book.

Many of the patterns included in this edition of *Flies of the Northwest* are relatively new. Some were created by innovative fly fishers and guides in the last few years. We have provided tiers and fly fishers with many patterns they might not find in other books, as well as patterns that have stood the test of time. All the patterns have been tested thoroughly by seasoned fly fishers.

Club Projects

The Inland Empire Fly Fishing Club is committed to enhancing the sport of fly-fishing in the Pacific Northwest. The club works closely with Trout Unlimited and the Federation of Fly Fishers. Its members also work with the Washington Department of Fish and Wildlife and in 1992 received the State of Environmental Excellence Award from the Washington State Ecological Commission for the club's participation with the Department of Fish and Wildlife in building a spawning bed in a stream feeding a small selective fishery.

Other projects funded by the profits from *Flies of the Northwest* include the effort to plug a leaking lake; improvement of the channel and banks of a spring creek; the installation of a spawning trap for the collection and stripping of egg-bound fish; and assisting the Department of Fish and Wildlife in planting trout in lakes and rivers.

How to Use This Book

*T*his book is organized to help new and experienced fly anglers and tiers find information on flies for specific insect orders, fish species or for general-purpose situations. Ultimately, we hope that it will increase the reader's angling knowledge and enjoyment of this sometimes frustrating activity called fly-fishing.

Each chapter has an introduction that gives an overview of the chapter. Angling techniques that are commonly used for a number of flies within the chapter are discussed in the overview rather than with each pattern. We suggest that the reader review the introductory pages and refer back to them when necessary.

If the reader wishes to study a subject more fully, the books listed in "References" can be consulted.

Hooks

Hooks are frequently a source of confusion, especially for new fly tiers. The originator of a fly pattern will often specify a certain hook for the pattern—and make convincing arguments for using it. Usually, however, other hooks will do the job well, and sometimes may be necessary to adapt to a particular situation. We reflect this by giving general hook specifications with the fly recipes and by providing a hook equivalency table to indicate the various manufacturers' model numbers which are suitable for the patterns. Only two hook models appear unique: Partridge Draper and Mustad Keel.

All others are categorized as dry, wet, scud, steelhead, or saltwater hooks. The category type and hook sizes listed for each pattern are followed by the length of the shank when it's longer than standard length. For example, a dry-fly hook in sizes 10-12 with a hook shank length equal to that normally found on a hook two to three times larger is listed as **Hook:** #10-12, Dry Fly, 2-3XL.

Dry-fly hooks are usually made with light gauge wire and have turned down eyes. Wet-fly hooks are made heavier than standard gauge and also have turned down eyes. Scud hooks have a "C" shaped, short shank. Steelhead hooks are often made with heavy gauge wire and turned up eyes. Saltwater hooks are usually nickel-plated, heavy gauge wire with turned down eyes. Straight eyes, up eyes, wide-gape hook-points, and various styles of bent shanks are common variables. *(See hook chart on page 126)*

Materials

Please note the order in which the materials are listed in the recipes. For each pattern, materials are given in the order in which they are tied on the hook—not in the order in which they're wrapped around the hook. For example, on many palmer-hackle flies the hackle is tied in before the body material. The body material is wound first, then the hackle is spiraled through it.

Pattern Variations

Many effective patterns also have variations or slight changes that better meet local needs. Variations are given in the text accompanying the recipe. Various styles of tying a particular pattern such as the use of bead heads, soft hackles, or parachute wings are pictured. These techniques can be incorporated into many different patterns in your search for the perfect fly.

All of the flies presented catch fish—and lots of them. If your flies do not look exactly like the pictures, use them anyway; the fish won't mind.

Bead–head Patterns

First introduced in the early 1990s, almost any nymph or wet-fly pattern can be turned into a bead-head pattern by threading a gold, silver, brass or multicolor bead onto the hook before tying on the other materials. Some tiers even put beads under the thorax or in the middle of the hook. Cone-shaped weights (coneheads) and tungsten beads (twice as heavy as brass) are available to enhance the patterns.

Soft–hackle Patterns

Soft-hackle flies can be traced to the origins of fly-fishing and they can be used to imitate almost any insect at nearly any stage, from larva to adult. These easily tied patterns require few materials. In many soft-hackle patterns a thorax of dubbing holds the soft barbs of the hackle away from the hook and enhances the tapered body shape.

In moving water, soft-hackle flies may be fished dead-drift, like a dry-fly, and a wet-fly swing at the end of the drift can be dynamite.

Examples of soft-hackle flies are found in the "Mayflies" section, page 16.

A Northwest Fly Fisher's Year

I t's not necessary for a fly fisher to carry scores of patterns in various sizes every time he or she fishes. Many veteran fly fishers, knowing what insects, crustaceans and minnows are active, carry relatively few patterns. Some even get along with one or two boxes of carefully chosen patterns.

The simplest way to select the flies you need is to note which insects hatch and how active crustaceans and minnows are each month of the year. Armed with this information, you won't have to invest in large numbers of patterns.

Before planning a fishing trip at any time of the year, it's best to consult local fly shops and obtain current information on fishing regulations, weather conditions, and recommendations for productive waters. A simple phone call or two can often make the difference between a great time and a wasted weekend.

January and February

Weather permitting, adventuresome fly fishers can often find a place to cast a line throughout the dead of winter. During January and February midges are about the only insects hatching in open water. Because water temperatures are in the 30s, trout are somewhat lethargic. However, trout, being opportunists, will take what's available, including imitations of midge pupae, scuds, dragonfly and damselfly nymphs, leeches and minnows.

During the first two months of the year, most of the Northwest's lakes are ice-capped, although lowland lakes of the Columbia Basin in eastern Washington and some coastal lakes in Washington and Oregon, may be ice-free and worth fishing during mild winters.

Recommended flies: Black Swannundaze Chironomid, #16; Palomino Midge, #20;

Brassie, #20; Serendipity, #18-20; Gold Ribbed Hare's Ear Nymph, #14 and #16; Clipped Scud, #16; Woolly Bugger, #8 2XL; Jolly Green Giant, #8 2XL; and Mohair Leech, #8 2XL.

The Swannundaze suggests Chironomid pupae. The Hare's Ear is an all-purpose nymph that can suggest everything from a scud to a mayfly nymph. Scuds are active the year-around, and a good scud imitation is an excellent searching fly. The Woolly Bugger and the Mohair Leech are effective leech patterns. Fish apparently take the Jolly Green Giant for a dragonfly nymph.

Streams are either closed or too cold to provide good fly-fishing the first two months of the year. A few Northwest spring creeks may offer good fly-fishing in January. Water temperatures in spring creeks flow out of the ground in the mid-50 degree range, and when air temperatures are below freezing, drop about 10 degrees in the first mile. Most trout remain in the warmer, upper sections of spring creeks during these winter months.

Baetis mayflies hatch at some streams throughout the winter, so most fly fishers carry a few patterns like the Blue-Winged Sparkle Dun, #18. Other effective patterns for streams and spring creeks during January and February are #22-24 midge patterns, #16-20 Hare's Ear Nymphs, #12-14 Clipped Scuds and #10-16 black Swannundaze Chironomids.

January and February are often the best months of the year for winter steelhead fishing in many coastal streams of the Pacific Northwest. The winter steelhead season extends from late November into May.

Recommended flies: Many steelheaders have a favorite fly, but most will tell you success comes to those who get the fly right in front of the fish's nose, especially in cold water or when water clarity is diminished. In cold, clear water, small bright flies are often the only thing that will move fish. In many of the coastal streams, shrimp-colored patterns do well. Large dark flies are the most visible and productive in dirty water conditions. Various combinations of sinking lines and weighted flies may be necessary to find willing winter steelhead.

March

Mild March days can bring on good midge hatches at Northwest lakes and fair hatches of *Baetis* mayflies in numerous streams. This is the month when many Northwest fly fishers converge on the numerous early-opening lakes of the Columbia Basin in eastern Washington. If water temperatures are in the high 40s or even the low 50s and Chironomids and leeches are active, anglers have a good opportunity to hook and release a few hungry trout. Effective patterns include the black Swannundaze Chironomid and Chan's Chironomid, #14 and #16, and the black Woolly Bugger, #6-8, 2-3XL.

Trout in some Montana rivers start feeding on hatching midges, stoneflies, and mayflies. Fly fishers hope weather conditions will allow their season to get under way along some blue-ribbon streams by mid-March. One of the more productive pre-runoff hatches is the emergence of the *Skwala* stonefly. Big trout readily take low-profile imitations along Montana's Clark Fork and Bitterroot rivers. This hatch also occurs in many eastern Oregon streams. The fly can be imitated by a #8 Riverbend Olive Stone or a #8 Olive Stimulator.

When the water temperature of Montana rivers rises above 45 degrees F, midges start hatching in massive numbers, and the hatch continues through late April. By then, major hatches of the other aquatic insects have usually started. The Palomino Midge has become the pattern of choice among many Northwest fly fishers who fish midge hatches.

April

Nearly all Northwest lakes are ice-free by the middle of April and those that are open to fishing provide excellent fly-fishing when Chironomids (midges) hatch. Midge hatches peak at many southeast Washington lakes in April, and a little later at most Montana and British Columbia lakes.

The Northwest's stream fishers look forward to fly-fishing several Montana streams before the spring runoff, which usually starts in late April. March Brown mayflies start hatching along numerous rivers in Montana, Idaho, and Oregon during the month. A #12 brown Sparkle Dun is one of the most effective patterns to imitate the March Brown, but even a #12 black-winged Green Drake pattern will deceive rainbow and brown trout during

A Northwest Fly Fisher's Year

a March Brown hatch. The *Skwala* and March Brown hatches usually peak in most Northwest rivers during April, but once the spring runoff begins the outstanding dry-fly fishing ends.

The large, brownish *Callibaetis* mayflies start hatching at many of the Northwest's low-land lakes during April. However, the biggest hatches occur during May at many lakes and during June or even July in the high altitude stillwaters. When these mayflies hatch, trout gorge themselves on the nymphs, duns, and even the spinners. Productive patterns during these *Callibaetis* hatches are the #14 Chopaka May, #14 tan Sparkle Dun and #12 and #14 Halfback.

May

The most satisfying time of year for some Northwest fly fishers starts in May and continues through June. *Callibaetis* mayflies, Chironomids, damselflies, dragonflies and caddisflies hatch at many lakes, providing for outstanding fly-fishing. Massive damselfly hatches are not uncommon. Productive damselfly nymph patterns are the #10 Damselfly Nymph and the #12 Back Pack Damsel. Dragonflies also hatch in large numbers. Good choices to imitate the dragonfly nymph are a #8, 2XL Ed Wolfe's Dragon Nymph or a #8, 2XL Jolly Green Giant.

Caddisflies start hatching at many stillwaters, including the highly productive British Columbia trout lakes. A type of caddisfly known as a "traveling sedge" hatches in numerous Canadian stillwaters, triggering occasional feeding frenzies. A #10 or #8 Olive Stimulator or a Mikulak Sedge in the same sizes provoke hard strikes by the high-jumping, native Kamloops rainbows.

Baetis, Pale Morning Dun and Green Drake mayflies, as well as caddisflies and stoneflies, hatch in streams. There is a downside for stream fly fishers. Some streams are still too high and off color in May for good fly-fishing. In fact, some years a few streams remain high through June and into July.

The first of the giant salmonflies start hatching in Montana in late May. Popular and productive patterns for the adult salmonfly are a #4 Improved Sofa Pillow or MacSalmon in large sizes. The Montana Nymph and Kaufmann's Black Stone tied on #4, long-shank hooks are excellent nymph imitators.

Pale Morning Dun mayflies become important to fly fishers in May. The PMDs start hatching along many north Idaho streams and along Montana rivers such as the Firehole, Madison and Clark Fork in early May. A #16 PMD Sparkle Dun or a Pale Morning Dun are productive patterns for PMD hatches.

June

Hatches of mayflies, damselflies, dragonflies, Chironomids, and caddisflies continue at Northwest stillwaters, and stonefly, caddisfly, and mayfly hatches peak at thousands of streams. The Madison River's famed salmonfly hatch usually starts in late June and continues through mid-July and the Henry's Fork Green Drake hatch begins about June 20 and ends in early July. Effective patterns during the latter hatch are a #12 or #10 Green Drake Paradrake and a Green Drake Emerger in the same sizes. Several other Montana rivers and some Idaho streams have good Green Drake hatches.

The PMD comes into its own in June, with hatches occurring on many Montana, Idaho, and Oregon streams. The hatches continue through August.

Massive caddisfly hatches take place in Northwest streams in June. One of the most productive patterns for various hatches is the Elk Hair Caddis. Many fly fishers use only this pattern when they fish Idaho and Montana rivers during June and July. Also productive is the X-Caddis. The Cased Caddis and Cactus Caddis patterns in sizes 10 to 14 are excellent flies for deep-water fishing.

July

Fly-fishing at most lowland lakes becomes restricted to early morning and late evening as temperatures rise. Many of the high elevation mountain lakes remain cool and can be productive throughout the summer.

With the advent of hot weather, most fly fishers turn their attention to moving waters as grasshoppers and other terrestrials become active. Many veteran fly fishers use the Madam X exclusively when hoppers are on the water. Another pattern that has become popular is the Turck's Tarantula, created in the Jackson Hole, Wyo. area, to suggest hoppers.

Foam beetle and ant patterns have become popular in recent years. Examples of productive foam patterns are included in this book. Veteran fly fishers often use beetle or ant patterns when they're not sure what the fish are taking.

Caddisflies and many mayflies continue to hatch in most Northwest moving waters. Active mayfly groups include PMDs, *Baetis*, Green and Brown Drakes, Flavs, *Callibaetis*, and Tricos. An outstanding Trico pattern is the Missouri River Trico in sizes 20 to 24. Tricos start hatching along the Missouri about the third week of July and continue hatching through October. Prime time is from the second week of August through the first week of September. Tricos hatch along the Madison from the second week of July through mid-September and from about mid-July through the second week of September along the Henry's Fork.

August

Most veteran fly fishers think of August as hopper season. So do trout, and for good reason. August is the month when hopper populations are at their peak along most Northwest rivers. Numerous hopper patterns are productive, including Jay-Dave's Hopper and Roope's Hopper.

During the summer, water levels drop and temperatures in many rivers and streams rise above the 60° to 65° Fahrenheit range. As water temperatures rise, the dissolved oxygen content in the water decreases. When oxygen levels are low, trout congregate in riffles to take advantage of the turbulent mixing of air and water, which temporarily increases the oxygen content. The extra oxygen allows fish to maintain higher levels of activity, including feeding. Anglers often do well in these areas, but should avoid over-playing trout during high water temperature conditions.

Trico and Pale Morning Dun mayflies and caddisflies continue to hatch at many streams during this month. However, many fly fishers find nymphs and streamers to be more productive. Patterns like the Bead Head Prince Nymph, Bead Head Hare's Ear Nymph, and Bead Head Pheasant Tail Nymph are popular. They're often fished under indicators. The Muddler Minnow and Woolhead Sculpin are effective streamer patterns.

Fishing is usually slow at stillwaters. Most insects have hatched and trout feed on tiny crustaceans, leeches, and the few damselfly and dragonfly nymphs they can find.

For many fly fishers, August marks the beginning of the summer-run steelhead season. Although summer-run steelhead begin entering freshwater rivers in June and July, their numbers are not large enough to attract the attention of most anglers until later in the summer and early fall. During summer months, steelheaders search for fish in cool water tributaries of the lower Columbia River and several streams on Vancouver Island, B.C.

Most summer-run steelheaders carry numerous patterns, but a few floaters and sinking flies, in sizes 2 and 4, usually take the fish. Productive dry flies include the Riffle Dancer, Waller Waker, and Bomber. One of the all-time favorite streamer patterns is the Green-Butt Skunk. Other good patterns are the Purple Peril, Black and Orange, and Marabou Spey.

September

Many fly fishers love September. Trout in both stillwaters and streams become more aggressive in response to decreasing daylight. Caddisflies and midges, as well as Gray Drakes,

Mahogany Duns, and Trico mayflies, actively hatch and hoppers are still around. The Mahogany Dun is a true fall mayfly that hatches along the Clark Fork, Gallatin, Henry's Fork and other streams. A #16 Mahogany Dun is a good imitation of the mayflies occurring at this time of year.

As water temperatures begin to cool, steelhead continue their migration up the Columbia River and its tributaries. They can also be found in several British Columbia river systems as well as various rivers in Alaska. Steelhead runs in most areas continue to decline at a time when the number of fly anglers pursuing them is increasing.

In September, water temperatures in most rivers are warm enough for steelheaders to use dry lines and dry or wet flies at the surface.

October

Like the preceding month, insect hatches in general continue to decline as water temperatures fall in both still and moving waters. Trout, however, remain quite active and feed at every opportunity as long as the weather holds. Anglers should not be too hasty in putting away their tackle and should take advantage of every warm autumn day.

Midges, Tricos, and caddisflies hatch along many streams and Chironomids can still be active in many lakes. Most fly fishers, however, resort to scud, dragonfly nymph, and leech patterns at stillwaters.

Many fly fishers have found water boatmen and backswimmer patterns to be very effective during the fall months. These insects are present throughout the year and are particularly active during spring and fall. With few other insects hatching during the fall, boatmen and backswimmers are eagerly sought out by trout cruising the shorelines of many lakes. Effective patterns are listed in the "Aquatic Bugs" chapter on page 70.

Summer-run steelhead fishing peaks during October in the upper Columbia River, Snake River, Skeena River and their tributaries. Warm days and cool nights produce ideal conditions for fly fishers. Most rivers and streams are in good condition and the only problem most steelheaders may face are weekend crowds. Wet and surface flies continue to produce fish.

November

This month often marks the end of the fly-fishing year for most trout anglers, except for the diehards we all know. Regulation closures and weather limit angling opportunities. A few insects may hatch sporadically on warmer days, but most anglers venturing out in November rely on midge pupae, scuds, dragonfly nymphs, crayfish, and boatmen patterns in stillwaters. Spring creeks may offer reasonable fishing for those who prefer moving waters.

November can be a very productive month for those fly fishers who choose to ignore the coming winter, defying ice and snow, redefining the term "steelhead" to simply reflect their state of mind. If nothing else, there usually are fewer anglers standing in your favorite run. Most steelhead are now taken on subsurface flies using a dry, sink-tip or sinking line.

December

Rare occasions allow fly fishers the opportunity to fish for trout during this month. Again midge pupae, scuds, dragonfly nymphs, and leech patterns are effective for any stillwaters remaining ice-free. Some spring creeks may provide moving water opportunities. Low water temperatures usually bring summer-run steelheading to a close on inland waterways. Winter steelhead begin showing up in many coastal streams in November, and December can be one of the more productive months, depending upon water temperatures and clarity. Wet flies and sinking lines are usually required.

Caution should be used during winter months by those venturing out into an unforgiving environment, as hypothermia becomes an ever-present threat.

Mayflies

Duns

Spinners

Nymphs

To fly fishers, the most important mayfly species in Northwest streams and lakes are the Blue-winged Olive (*Baetis*), Trico (*Tricorythodes*), Western March Brown (*Rhithrogena morrisoni*), Pale Morning Dun (*Ephemerella inermis* and *infrequens*), Green Drake (*Drunella*) and Speckle-Wing Quill (*Callibaetis*). The first five are found in a high percentage of streams in Oregon, Washington, Idaho, Montana, and British Columbia. The sixth, the *Callibaetis*, is the most important stillwater mayfly.

Numerous other mayfly species hatch in the Northwest, but for one reason or another, they're not quite as important to fly fishers as those prolific six. Hatches of other species are generally sparse or sporadic.

Most fly fishers who regularly fish certain streams and stillwaters carry patterns that simulate the nymphs, emergers, duns, and spinners of the major mayfly species that inhabit those waters.

Mayfly patterns in this chapter simulate various stages of the Blue-winged Olives, Pale Morning Duns, Tricos, Green Drakes, March Browns, and Speckle-winged Quills. Some patterns, including the Adams, Hare's Ear Nymph, and Pheasant Tail Nymph, are all-purpose or impressionistic flies that are used to imitate several different species. A few are attractor patterns.

Mayflies start their lives as nymphs, hatch into duns (sub-imago), and then molt into spinners (imago). Duns have dull body and wing color; spinners have shiny bodies and transparent wings. The body color of adult mayflies is darker on top than on the underbelly. Therefore, it's necessary to look at the undersurface of these insects to appreciate a trout's perspective of the bug's coloring. As full-grown adults, mayflies have short lives, in some cases less than a day.

Knowing something about mayfly nymphs can help a fly fisher identify a species. Mayfly nymphs are classified as swimmers, crawlers, clingers, and burrowers.

Swimmers

Nymphs of the Blue-winged Olive and Speckle-winged Quill mayflies are classified as swimmers. They're slender and quite active. In the water they dart around aquatic plants. Their three tails are fringed with interlocking hairs that help propel them. When fly fishers use nymph patterns of these two species, they often employ short strips to simulate the swimming movements of the nymphs.

Blue-winged Olive nymphs range in color from light tan to dark brown, depending on their surroundings, and are about 1/4- to 1/2-inch long, excluding the length of their tails. Patterns to simulate them are tied on size 14 to 20 hooks. The duns are about the same length as the nymphs. The duns have two tails, wings of blue dun or slate gray and bodies that range in color from light olive to dark olive or brownish gray. The spinners have two tails and light brown to reddish brown bodies.

Blue-winged Olives hatch from late February to November, depending on the location. They're considered basic mayflies along many rivers, including the Missouri and other Montana streams and the Henry's Fork in Idaho. Because Blue-winged Olives hatch over a period of several months, most anglers who fish streams have good supplies of duns, emergers, and nymphs.

The Speckle-wing mayflies, like the *Callibaetis*, are active swimmers and are the most important stillwater mayflies in the Northwest. Although they primarily hatch in lakes, *Callibaetis* mayflies are also abundant in some slow-moving streams, including the Missouri and Henry's Fork. They hatch from early spring until fall. For example, the mayflies start hatching at many eastern Washington lakes in April and at many Montana lakes, including Hebgen in the West Yellowstone area, through August and into September.

All three stages of the species are important to fly fishers. The nymphs—gray, tan, grayish brown or pale green—are 1/4- to 1/2-inch long. The duns, which have two tails, mottled wings and underbodies that usually range from tan to olive, bring big trout to the surface. Trout sometimes will take spinners as readily as duns, but because it is so difficult to compete with the carpet of spent spinners covering the water's surface, relatively few fly fishers carry patterns to simulate *Callibaetis* spinners.

Callibaetis nymphs are active swimmers, so fly fishers imitate their swimming motion by short, start-stop strips of their lines.

Crawlers

Pale Morning Dun, Green Drake and Trico mayfly nymphs are classified as crawlers. The robust nymphs crawl over stream bottoms and, when dislodged, swim feebly, wiggling their abdomens up and down. Because the nymphs are poor swimmers, patterns representing them are usually fished dead-drift.

Each stage of a Pale Morning Dun hatch can provide exciting fishing. The 1/4- to 3/8-inch PMD nymphs, which are readily available to trout as they ascend to the surface, have three yellowish amber tails, abdomens and thoraxes of chartreuse or pale yellow, and gray wing pads. The duns, which are of the same length, have light bluish gray wings, three tails, and bodies that can be pale yellow with an olive sheen, yellow-orange or even mahogany, the color depending on gender or stream. Some PMDs on the Missouri have a pinkish cast.

The Henry's Fork is famous for its Green Drake hatches, but all four subspecies of this big mayfly hatch along numerous Northwest streams. These mayflies hatch somewhere in the Northwest from June through September.

The most important Green Drake mayfly on the Henry's Fork is the *Drunella grandis*. It isn't important for a fly fisher to identify a subspecies to select a pattern. The size and color of the bugs that are present are the most important factors when choosing a fly.

Green Drake nymphs are 1/8 to 3/4 inches long, have three tails, and generally range from shades of brown to olive-brown in color. The duns have three tails, dark slate-gray to yellowish wings, and bright olive-green to pale cream or yellowish tan bodies. The spinners

Mayflies

have clear wings, three tails, and slender bodies that range from brown to dark olive-green to pale cream or tan.

Massive hatches of the minute Tricos occur from spring to late fall on numerous Northwest rivers, including the Henry's Fork, Clark Fork, Missouri, and Madison. The 1/8- to 1/2-inch long, three-tailed nymph is seldom imitated. The dun and spinner stages are the most important phases for fly fishers. The 1/8- to 1/4-inch long, three-tailed duns have whitish wings. The female duns have light green abdomens and dark brown thoraxes; both the abdomens and thorax of the males are dark brown. The spinners have three tails and clear wings. Female spinners have green abdomens and brown thoraxes; males have dark brown or black abdomens and thoraxes. Most Trico patterns are tied on size 20 to 24 hooks.

Clingers

One species of the Western March Brown starts hatching along Oregon rivers, including the Deschutes and McKenzie, in late February and continues hatching until early April. A hatch on the Henry's Fork usually starts the third week of May. Other species hatch in June, July,

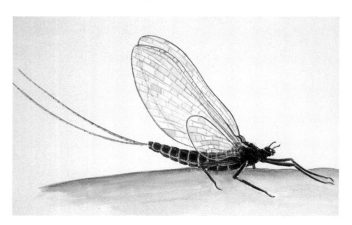

and August. This mayfly is fairly large and imitations of it are usually tied on sizes 12 to 16 hooks.

The wide, flat, 1/8- to 1/2-inch-long March Brown nymphs are classified as clingers. They cling tenaciously to smooth stones and they're seldom available to trout. However, when they are ready to emerge, they let go of the rocks and swim feebly toward the surface. That's the time when nymph patterns become important. Fly fishers drift their patterns along the bottom. Nymph imitations are usually tied on size 12 and 14 hooks. The nymphs have olive-brown to dark brown bodies.

The two-tailed duns have mottled brown wings and olive, cream, tan, or light brown underbodies. The clear-winged, two-tailed spinners have tan to light brown underbodies. Duns, usually tied on sizes 12 to 16 hooks, emerge in the afternoons and early evening.

Other Mayflies

Other Northwest hatches of significant local interest include Flavs (*Drunella flavilinea*), Gray Drake (*Siphlonurus occidentalis*), Mahogany Duns (*Paraleptophlebia*), Little Yellow May (*Epeorus*) and Pale Evening Dun (*Heptagenia*), and the Sand Fly or Big Yellow May (*Hexagenia limbata*).

The Big Yellow May nymph is a burrower. Significant hatches of the Big Yellow May occur in Oregon and along the Columbia River, and they have been reported in Idaho and Montana. However, these big mayflies, 1 1/2 inches long, hatch at night so few anglers are aware of them.

The Brown Drake (*Ephemera simulans*), White Drake (*Ephoron album*) and White Mayfly (*Ephoron leukon*) are also burrowers.

The following books are good sources of information on mayflies that hatch in the Northwest: *The Complete Book of Western Hatches*, by Rick Hafele and Dave Hughes; *Handbooks of Hatches*, by Dave Hughes; *Fishing Yellowstone Hatches*, by John Juracek and Craig Mathews; *Mayflies, the Angler and the Trout*, by Fred L. Arbona Jr., and *Micropatterns*, by Darrel Martin. *The Soft-Hackled Fly,* by Sylvester Nemes provides useful information on soft-hackle fishing techniques and patterns often used to simulate mayflies.

Baetis

Blue–Winged Olive Sparkle Dun

Hook: #16-22, Dry Fly
Thread: Olive 6/0-8/0
Shuck: Olive-brown Z-lon
Abdomen and Thorax: Dark olive
Wing: Gray deer hair

Originators: Craig Mathews and John Juracek, West Yellowstone, Mont.

This durable pattern sits on and in the surface film. Trout accept the fly as an adult or a mayfly that's still hatching or has been stillborn. The Z-lon should be one-half to the full length of the hook shank. Originators call for polypropylene dubbing. Various colors and sizes of this sparkle-dun-style fly can be used to imitate many other mayflies.

Baetis Floating Nymph

Hook: #16-26, Dry Fly
Thread: Olive 8/0
Tail: Hackle fibers
Body and Thorax: Olive dubbing
Rib: Olive 6/0-8/0 thread
Wingcase: Gray dubbing ball
Legs: Stiff hackle fibers

Originators: Doug Swisher and Don Richards

Body colors for this simple fly include olive-brown, olive-gray and gray, depending on the stream. Fly fishers should collect *Baetis* nymphs from the streams they fish to determine the right body color. This simple pattern is effective wherever *Baetis* mayflies hatch. Grease only the wingcase and use the fly as the duns start emerging. *Baetis* nymphs are often simulated with Pheasant Tail Nymphs and Hare's Ear Nymphs.

Thread Body *Baetis* Soft Hackle

Hook: #14-18, Dry Fly, 2-3XL
Thread: Olive 6/0-8/0
Tail: Z-lon fibers
Rib: Yellow thread
Body: Olive thread
Hackle and Wing: Starling hackle

This method of using a hackle tip to form a wing is called the Glanrhos style. The first fly tied in this manner has been attributed to L.J. Graham Clarke, who owned the Glanrhos Water on the Wye, a salmon river in Wales. The pattern represents emerging *Baetis* nymphs.

Mayflies

Biot/Starling Soft Hackle

Hook: #14-18, Dry Fly, 2XL
Thread: Green 6/0-8/0
Rib: Green thread doubled
Body: Goose biot
Hackle: Starling

Sylvester Nemes has written several books dealing with tying and fishing traditional soft-hackle flies. He is credited with the rebirth in popularity of this early form of fly-fishing. Many game birds, crow, starling, and woodcock provide the small round or oval feathers needed for the soft-hackle collars. These simple patterns imitate many insect species. The pattern shown suggests a *Baetis* mayfly nymph.

Biot Nymph

Hook: #16-26, Dry Fly, 2XL
Thread: Olive 8/0
Body: Olive goose biot
Thorax: Peacock herl

This pattern became popular in the Northwest after Edward Thomas of Billings, Mont., demonstrated at a Federation of Fly Fishers conclave how the fly is tied. The pattern suggests the nymph of a *Baetis* mayfly. The goose biot body seems to be ideal to suggest the body of the *Baetis* nymph.

Pheasant Tail Nymph

Hook: #10-20, Wet Fly
Thread: Black or brown 6/0-8/0
Tail: Pheasant tail wisps
Rib: Copper wire
Body: Pheasant tail fibers
Thorax: Peacock herl
Wingcase: Pheasant tail fibers
Legs: Wingcase fiber tips

This western version of Sawyer's Pheasant Tail Nymph is a must pattern for Northwest rivers. Extremely effective when several mayfly nymph species are active, the pattern also can be used to imitate caddisflies and midges on both rivers and lakes. The pattern can be weighted by flattening fine diameter wire and wrapping it around the hook shank.

Callibaetis

Callibaetis Compara–dun

Hook: #12-18, Dry Fly
Thread: Brown 8/0
Tail: Gray Z-lon
Wing: Light coastal deer hair
Body: Gray/brown fur, dubbing

The *Callibaetis* mayfly is the most prevalent mayfly in Northwest stillwaters. Several generations of these mayflies hatch at low elevation waters, each generation smaller than the previous one. The body and wing colors should match the duns that hatch where the fly fisher plans to fish.

Chopaka May

Hook: #14-18, Dry Fly
Thread: Gray 6/0
Tail: Moose body hair
Body: Gray polypropylene
Wing: Single, upright deer hair
Hackle: Dun

Originator: Boyd Aigner, Seattle, Wash.
This pattern was created to simulate *Callibaetis* mayflies that hatch in many Northwest lakes and slow-moving water. Aigner's first versions were used at Montana lakes. Clip the hackles across the bottom to make the pattern ride upright.

Gray Quill

Hook: #12-16, Dry Fly
Thread: Black 6/0
Tail: Grizzly hackle fibers
Body: Grizzly hackle quill
Wing: Teal or pintail flank fibers
Hackle: Grizzly

Originator: Walt Balek, Spokane, Wash.
This pattern was originated in the early 1980s to imitate the *Callibaetis* mayfly. The wing is a single post of teal or pintail flank feathers. Reinforce quill body with head cement. Since several generations of *Callibaetis* hatch each summer, a fly fisher should carry the pattern in sizes 12 to 16.

Parachute Adams

Hook: #10-22, Dry Fly
Thread: Black 6/0-8/0
Tail: Grizzly hackle fibers
Body: Gray muskrat
Post: White poly
Hackle: Grizzly and brown

Originator: Leonard Halladay, Mayfield, Mich.

The standard Adams is one of the most widely used and productive fly patterns ever created. It can simulate a variety of mayflies and even hatching midges. The Parachute Adams, tied with the same materials and a white poly or fine calf tail post, is just about as popular as the standard Adams. To create an egg-laying female mayfly, add a butt of yellow poly dubbing.

Halfback

Hook: #8-14, Wet Fly, 2-3XL
Thread: Black or olive 6/0
Tail: Pheasant tail tips
Rib: Fine gold wire
Body: Peacock herl
Wingcase: Pheasant tail fibers
Legs: Tips of wingcase fibers
(Continued on page 22)

Mayflies

(Halfback continued from page 21)
The Halfback, created in Canada, is an imitation of the *Callibaetis* mayfly nymph. The thorax is tied thicker than the abdomen. Brown rump feathers can also be used to tie the wing-case. The ribbing should be wrapped counter to the herl wrap. A popular variation is the Fullback, tied essentially the same except that 4XL hooks are used and the wingcase is extended the full length of the body. The pattern also takes fish when damselfly nymphs are moving.

Pheasant Tail Soft Hackle

Hook: #22-26, Dry Fly
Thread: Red 8/0
Rib: Fine gold wire
Body: Pheasant tail fibers
Hackle: Partridge

This variation of the Pheasant Tail Nymph is tied with a short body on a large hook. Using a hook that is one size larger proportionally enhances hooking ability. The partridge hackle opens and closes as the pattern is retrieved, giving the fly a lifelike appearance.

Hexagenia limbata

Hexagenia Paradrake

Hook: #10-16, Dry Fly
Thread: Yellow 6/0
Tail: Yellow elk hair
Body: Yellow elk hair
Wing: Yellow elk hair
Hackle: Yellow-dyed grizzly

The *Hexagenia limbata,* often called the Big Yellow May, hatches at some Northwest lakes and slow-moving streams. It is a nocturnal mayfly, usually hatching after sunset but sometimes during late, cloudy afternoons. The dun is one of the largest mayflies in North America. Because the mayfly hatches at night, relatively few fly fishers realize that trout feed actively on the big nymphs, and duns of 1 1/2 inches.

Hexagenia Nymph

Hook: #4-8, Wet Fly, 2-3XL
Thread: Pale yellow 6/0
Tail: Gray marabou
Rib: Copper wire
Back: Dark turkey quill
Gills: Gray pheasant filoplume
Abdomen and Thorax: Yellow rabbit
Legs: Mottled hen saddle

The big nymph lives burrowed in mud and is vulnerable to fish as it swims to the surface to hatch. Because it has prominent gills along the sides of its body, this pattern incorporates the frequently discarded pheasant filoplumes to simulate the gills. Filoplumes produce a lifelike action under water. The pattern often is weighted for use along slow-moving streams.

Bead Head Mayfly Nymph

Hook: #14-18, 2XL
Thorax: Gold bead
Thread: Maroon 6/0-8/0
Tail: Wood duck or dyed mallard
Rib: Gold or copper wire
Abdomen: Antron dubbing
Wingcase: Natural duck or goose
Legs: Brown partridge

This pattern is similar to the Hendrickson nymph described in *The Fly Tyers Nymph Manual,* by Randall Kaufmann, except that the dubbed thorax is replaced with a gold bead. Both patterns are designed to imitate the PMD nymph. The dubbing can be olive, tan or brown to match the color of the nymph being imitated. Legs of brown partridge should be divided.

Mahogany Dun

Mahogany Dun

Hook: #16, Dry Fly
Thread: Brown 6/0
Tail (shuck): Brown Z-lon
Body: Brown dubbing
Wing: Natural deer hair

This sparkle dun pattern was popularized by John Juracek and Craig Mathews of West Yellowstone, Mont. The Mahogany Dun mayfly hatches sporadically during the summer at many Northwest streams. The biggest hatches occur in September and early October in the West Yellowstone area and in other parts of Montana. The duns have mahogany colored bodies, dark gray wings and three tails.

Mahogany Dun Fur Nymph

Hook: #16, Dry Fly
Thread: Brown 8/0
Tail: Brown partridge fibers
Body: Brown dubbing
Wingcase: Gray polycelon
Thorax: Same as body, picked out

Originators: John Juracek and Craig Mathews, West Yellowstone, Mont.

Juracek and Mathews say in their book, *Fishing Yellowstone Hatches,* that they usually fish with a nymph imitation during a Mahogany Dun hatch. Mahogany Duns generally emerge from mid-morning until early afternoon. The mayfly starts coming out in September and is the last fairly large mayfly to hatch in the late fall at many Northwest streams.

Mayflies

Gold Ribbed Hare's Ear

Hook: #6-22, Wet Fly
Thread: Brown or black 6/0-8/0
Tail: Hare's mask guard hairs
Rib: Gold wire or tinsel
Body: Dubbed hare's mask
Wingcase: Dark raffia
Thorax: Dark hare's mask, picked out

This is one of several different versions of the widely popular Gold Ribbed Hare's Ear Nymph. Nearly all experienced fly fishers carry their versions of the pattern in several different sizes. The fly represents mayfly nymphs, caddisfly pupae and even freshwater shrimp. Many fly fishers automatically tie on a Hare's Ear Nymph as a searching pattern.

March Brown

March Brown

Hook: #12-18, Dry Fly
Thread: Dark brown 8/0
Tail: Brown hackle fibers
Rib: Fine copper wire
Body: Brown dubbing
Wings: Brown hen neck tips
Hackle: Brown

The brown body is tapered from relatively fine near the tail to nearly double that diameter in the thorax area. Some tiers clip the hackle so that it's even with the bottom of the body, ensuring that the pattern will sit upright in the water. March Brown mayflies that hatch along many Northwest streams early each year are so large that patterns are tied on No. 12 hooks.

Western March Brown Nymph

Hook: #12-14, Wet Fly, 2-3XL
Thread: Brown 6/0
Tail: 3 pheasant tail fibers
Underbody: Flattened wire
Rib: Fine gold wire
Abdomen: Pheasant tail fibers
Wingcase: Partridge wing
    fibers
Thorax: Hare's mask dubbing
Legs: Partridge flank fibers

Western March Brown mayflies sometimes hatch as early as February in Northwest streams. The biggest hatches occur in March, but some take place in April and May. Non-lead wire is wrapped on hook and flattened to simulate the flat body of the nymph. The nymph usually is fished dead drift. The partridge hackles (representing legs) are tied on top of the hook because the weighted pattern rides upside down.

Muddle May

Hook: #12-20, Dry Fly
Thread: Gray 6/0-8/0
Tail: Moose body hair, sparse
Body: Dubbed muskrat
Wings: Grizzly hackle, looped
Hackle: Deer hair
Head: Spun and trimmed

Originator: Al Beatty, Bozeman, Mont.
Beatty crossed the Adams and Muddler Minnow in developing this innovative pattern in 1985. It floats as well as a Humpy, but looks more like a mayfly. Fish it as a mayfly dun. The looped wing is normally tied with the stems of hackle tips. However, Beatty feels this makes the wing too stiff so he uses only the looped back hackle barbs. Usually tied on #14 and #16 light wire hooks.

Pale Morning Dun

PMD No Hackle

Hook: #14-24, Dry Fly
Thread: Light yellow 8/0
Tail: Ginger hackle fibers
Body: Pale olive fur
Wing: Badger hackle

Originator: John Propp, Spokane, Wash.
Massive hatches of Pale Morning Dun mayflies occur along most Northwest trout streams from May through September, though the duration of the hatch varies. Many fly fishers consider the Pale Morning Dun hatches to be

the most important mayfly hatches of the year. Although the insects are small, unbelievably thick hatches make up for their individual size. PMD bodies are pale yellow, with shades of olive.

Pale Morning Dun Nymph

Hook: #14-16, Wet Fly
Thread: Cream 6/0
Tail: Wood duck
Rib: Fine wire
Body: Gray or tan dubbing
Wingcase: Pheasant tail fibers

Originator: Walt Cubley, Spokane, Wash.
Cubley blends various dubbing furs, including gray, tan, pink, and wheat, to match bodies of Pale Morning Dun nymphs in the waters where he fishes. In designing the nymph, he took into consideration the fact that nymph colors vary considerably throughout the Northwest, even in different stretches of the same river.

PMD Soft Hackle

Hook: #14-18, Dry Fly
Thread: Olive 6/0-8/0
Tail: Clear Z-lon or sparkle poly
Body and Thorax: Yellow tan dubbing
Hackle: Cream or ginger hen

This fly is tied and used like many other of Sylvester Nemes' traditional soft-hackled patterns. This pattern can be fished dead-drift with a reach cast, or downstream and across for a sunken swing, or a combination of both. The thorax area is built up to hold the hackle away from the body and form a tapered body appearance in the water. Use only a few strands of Z-lon for the tail.

Green Drake

Green Drake Paradrake

Hook: #12-14, Dry Fly
Thread: Yellow 6/0
Wing: Dark elk hair
Tail: Moose body hair
Body and Thorax: Olive elk hair
Hackle: Yellow-olive grizzly

The tying style originated with Carl Richards and Doug Swisher, and was refined by Mike Lawson and Rene' Harrop. This extended-body Green Drake dun imitation was designed on the Henry's Fork and is now widely used wherever the large mayflies hatch. Some fly fishers tie the pattern in smaller sizes to imitate the Flav mayflies that hatch in large numbers along the Henry's Fork and other Northwest streams.

Green Drake Emerger

Hook: #8-12, Dry Fly, 2XL
Thread: Olive 3/0
Tail: Moose body hair
Rib: Yellow floss strand
Body: Olive, dubbed
Wing: Black elk body hair
Hackle: Olive-dyed grizzly

Originator: Mike Lawson, Last Chance, Ida.
Originated about 1971, this pattern is effective just before duns emerge. Treat the pattern with floatant and dead-drift it in the surface film, occasionally twitching it to simulate life. A blend of olive rabbit fur and a little Antron make a fine body. Moose body hair can be used for the wing. Hen neck is best for hackle.

Green Drake Nymph

Hook: #10-12, Wet Fly, 2XL
Thread: Olive 6/0
Tail: Olive-dyed mallard
Rib: Fine copper wire
Body: Blended olive hare's
  ear and Antron
Wingcase: Dark turkey tail
Hackle: Brown partridge

Originator: Mike Lawson,
Last Chance, Ida.
Mike Lawson developed
this pattern to fish during

the Green Drake hatch on the Henry's Fork. The large mayfly is slow and clumsy as it emerges, resulting in an easy meal for trout. Fish the pattern like any other emerger. Lawson prefers wood duck for the tail but specifies olive-dyed mallard as a substitute. The wingcase should be dark. Partridge hackle (for legs) are tied out to side.

All–purpose

Black Flashback

Hook: #10-18, Wet Fly
Thread: Black 6/0-8/0
Tail: Black pheasant tail
Rib: Medium gold wire
Wingcase: #10 flat silver tinsel
Thorax and Abdomen: Black
  dubbing

A guide gave a sample of this pattern to Tim Tollett of Dillon, Mont., during a fishing trip to New Zealand. Tollett, a sporting goods dealer, fished the pattern in the Northwest and then added it and other Flashback patterns to his catalog. As a result, Flashback patterns have become popular in Montana and other Northwest states.

Feather Duster

Hook: #8-12, Wet Fly, 2XL
Thread: Brown 6/0
Tail: Pheasant tail fibers
Rib: Fine gold wire
Body and Thorax: Gray
  ostrich herl
Wingcase: Pheasant tail
  fibers

Originator: Wally Eagle, West
Yellowstone, Mont.
The many versions of this

pattern, including those for steelhead, are tied with soft, fuzzy material like ostrich herl or marabou to provide lifelike, underwater movement. In small sizes, the ostrich herl simulates the gills of a mayfly. The body is smaller than the thorax. Wire for weight wrapped under the thorax is an option. A variation uses herl from a peacock eye for the wingcase, and a tail of lemon wood duck.

Mayflies

Quigley's Mayfly Cripple

Hook: #12-18, Dry Fly
Thread: Tan 6/0
Tail: Tan marabou
Abdomen: Stripped hackle stem
Thorax: Tan poly
Wing: Light tan deer hair
Hackle: Light ginger dun

Originator: Bob Quigley

Many mayfly nymphs fail to hatch into healthy duns and are easy prey for foraging fish. This is one of many patterns devised to simulate a crippled mayfly. Materials used should match the natural. The deer or elk hair should be tied so that it's pointing forward over the hook eye. Length of the hair shouldn't be longer than the body. Butt ends are trimmed short over the top of the thorax.

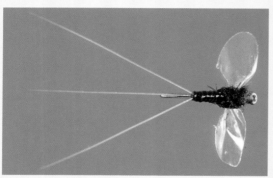

Missouri River Trico

Hook: #20-22, Dry Fly
Thread: Black 8/0
Tail: White microfibetts
Abdomen: Stripped peacock herl
Thorax: Fine black dubbing
Wings: Clear plastic, shaped

Originator: Arnie Gidlow, Craig, Mont.
This Trico pattern was developed by guide and outfitter Gidlow to simulate the tiny mayflies that hatch along the Missouri River. When fishing Trico patterns, casts should be short, numerous and, if possible, in a trout's feeding lane. Strikes often are hard as fish take a pattern and move away quickly. As a result, inexperienced fly fishers often break 6X tippets on the strike. Wide gap hooks are suggested.

Rusty CDC Spinner

Hook: #14-24, Dry Fly
Thread: Orange 6/0 or 8/0
Tail: Gray cock hackle fibers
Abdomen: Rusty brown goose biot
Wings: White CDC, white Z-lon
Thorax: Rusty brown dubbed

Originator: René Harrop, St. Anthony, Ida.
This is one of numerous patterns developed by Harrop and Co. calling for CDC feathers. Some tiers use rusty turkey biot for the body and rusty Superfine dubbing for the thorax. CDC feathers from ducks and geese are the feathers around a gland at the rear of the birds' bodies. Waterfowl waterproof their feathers with the oily secretion emitted from the gland. Many tiers also use soft CDC feathers for wet flies.

Chironomids

Adults

Pupae

Larvae

*I*f mayflies are the *pièce de résistance* to feeding trout in still and slow-moving waters, Chironomids are their bread and butter. Fly fishers often refer to Chironomids as midges.

Naturally, trout, being opportunists, eat everything from near-microscopic crustaceans to juicy leeches, but those food items aren't on their menu as often as Chironomid larvae, pupae, and adults. Chironomids hatch anytime the water isn't covered with ice.

At times, Chironomid hatches are massive. In Northwest waters, the biggest hatches occur during April, May, and June. Also during those months the largest Chironomids hatch. Chironomid pupae in many lakes, particularly those in British Columbia, are 3/4 to 1 1/4 inches long, making them choice morsels for hungry trout. Furthermore, they're extremely vulnerable to trout when they leave the bottom and slowly make their way to the surface of the water to hatch.

Not all Chironomid pupae are large. In fact, the average length probably is only about 1/2 inch long. However, fly fishers have learned that it's not necessary in most cases to use imitations that are exactly the length of the pupae that are hatching. Trout often will take imitations that are three-quarters of an inch long.

To fish Northwest stillwaters effectively, a fly fisher must carry a variety of patterns in hook sizes 8 to 18 that simulate the Chironomids that trout feed on.

Jack Shaw, author of *Fly Fish the Trout Lakes*, apparently was the first to realize the importance of Chironomid imitations and write about fishing with them. However, until Richard B. Thompson, a Washington fisheries biologist, developed the first popular Chironomid pupa imitation in the 1960s, few fly fishers realized that trout in stillwaters depend upon Chironomids for much of their food. Thompson's pattern wasn't an overnight

Chironomids

success. Even after he publicized his TDC (Thompson's Delectable Chironomid) Nymph in the spring 1963 issue of "Washington Game Department Game Bulletin," few fly fishers understood the significance of Chironomids in the diet of trout. Some tried the pattern, but didn't do well with it. What they didn't realize was that the fly had to be fished extremely slowly. When pupae start toward the surface to hatch, they move slowly, their bodies undulating. They stop periodically to rest. For trout, in the words of the Pentagon, a Chironomid hatch is a "target rich" environment.

Years passed after Thompson publicized his pattern before large numbers of fly fishers understood that Chironomid patterns must be retrieved dead slow.

Over time, innovative fly fishers developed new patterns to simulate Chironomid larvae, pupae, and adults. Some of the most effective patterns are included in this chapter.

Chironomids, members of the family Chironomidae, have a four-stage life cycle: Egg, larva, pupa, and adult. To the fly fisher, the pupa is the most important stage, but the larva and adult patterns can be productive at times.

Chironomid larvae are long, slender, worm-like, and have segmented bodies. The larvae of many species are bright red and are commonly known as "bloodworms." Other species are white, pink, blue, or yellow. Many species construct fragile tubes of algae, silt, or grains of sand around themselves. Fly fishers have developed a variety of patterns to simulate larvae.

Chironomid pupae also have long and segmented bodies. However, they are tapered, with the head considerably thicker than the tail. Wingcases are near the head, and the whitish gill filaments are at both the head and tail. Most pupae in Northwest waters are brownish black, but some have brownish, greenish, and reddish bodies.

The adults look like mosquitoes, but they don't bite. Mating swarms sometimes are so heavy that they cover windshields of cars that pass through them. They even fly into the mouths of anglers.

Chironomid hatches occur most of the year at Northwest stillwaters. Even in the winter, pupae will rise to the surface and hatch into adults wherever there is open water, and trout will feed on them.

Fly fishers expect big hatches to start occurring in late April and May in shallow, low-elevation lakes. In those lakes, water temperatures are usually high enough for good hatches by mid-May. At higher-elevation lakes, particularly those in British Columbia, hatches might not peak until June.

The most popular Chironomid pupae patterns in Northwest waters are the Swannundaze Chironomid and the Chan Chironomid. Dressings for these patterns are included in this book.

Fishing Techniques

Nearly all Northwest fly fishers use 9- to 10-foot graphite rods when fishing Chironomid patterns. Floating lines are usually used, but some fly fishers use intermediate, sink tip, and sinking lines. An intermediate line is an advantage when variable winds blow and create "S" curves in a floating line. The sink tip and sinking lines are used by some fly fishers when trout are feeding on Chironomid pupae in water 15 to 25 feet deep.

When fishing from boats, most veteran fly fishers anchor at both ends to keep their boats from swinging back and forth. It's difficult to detect delicate takes when a boat is moving and causing the line to curve.

Fly fishers who fish from float tubes or similar craft use only one anchor and try to keep their tubes from swinging around and causing "S" curves in their lines.

Strike indicators which, like bait anglers' bobbers, move or go under when a fish takes a fly, are popular with many fly fishers. However, some prefer to use long leaders and a countdown method to get their pupa patterns to the trouts' feeding depth. Some fly fishers mark anchor lines to determine water depths; some carry cord marked with permanent ink at foot-long intervals, and others, particularly those who fish out of boats, use sonar.

In stillwaters in Washington and Idaho, the majority of fly fishers use strike indicators. Some tie the indicators near the end of their lines; others attach them onto the tippet. When fishing in water that's less than eight feet deep, many fly fishers use small, highly visible chartreuse or orange indicators made of closed-cell foam or cork. These indicators are just large enough to remain afloat against the downward pull of a good-sized, weighted pupae pattern.

When fishing deep water, most fly fishers use polypropylene yarn indicators treated with a wax-like or liquid floatant. With these dressings, the indicator can go through rod guides easily. Eventually, though, these indicators will sink, making it necessary to change to a fresh one.

When trout are taking Chironomids, they usually remain near the bottom and interrupt the pupae as they start to rise to the surface. Consequently, most fly fishers determine the depth and fish their patterns a few inches off the bottom. Some fly fishers use long leaders, usually 12 to 18 feet long, to get their flies down and count as the fly sinks. If they hook a fish when the count goes to 20 seconds, on subsequent casts they'll count to 20 before starting a long, extremely slow retrieve. As results change, they'll adjust the count.

When fishing with Chironomids, fly fishers usually cast downwind, sometimes slightly to the side to permit the line to drift slowly to a straight-out position. When their pupa pattern is at the depth where they want it to be, many use a hand-twist retrieve, stopping frequently to simulate the upward movement and resting of the pupae. Trout often will take a pupa pattern while it is stationary.

When a hatch peaks, trout often feed on pupae that are hatching in the surface film. At such a time, many fly fishers like to fish pupae imitations tied on light wire hooks. Sometimes they put floatant on their leaders—to within a few inches of the fly.

The most successful Chironomid fly fishers concentrate on their fishing, knowing that trout frequently take a fly so delicately that the take can be overlooked, especially when the wind is blowing.

When a trout takes a pupae pattern, the fly fisher quickly raises his rod tip to set the hook. If the hook isn't set within a second or so, the trout will eject the pattern.

Eventually during a hatch, especially during weather cool enough to keep newly hatched Chironomids from flying for a few seconds, trout will feed on the adults. It's during those times that fly fishers tie on their floating patterns. Among the most productive are the Griffith's Gnat and Lady McConnel, patterns that are featured in this chapter.

Chironomids

Bead Head Chironomid

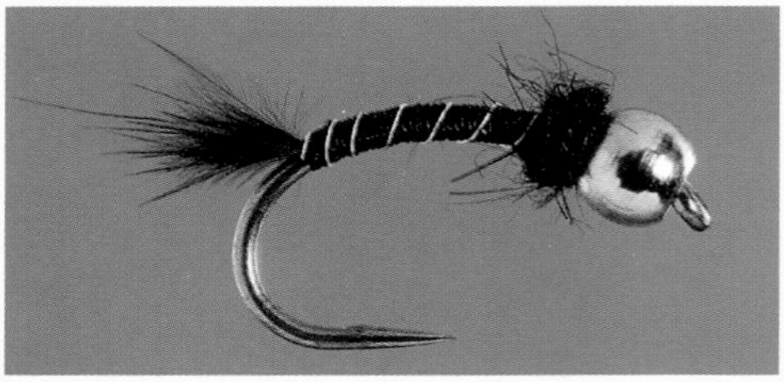

Hook: #8-12, Scud
Head: Metal bead
Thread: Black 6/0
Tail: Black filoplume
Rib: Fine gold wire
Body: Black Antron yarn
Thorax: Black dubbing

Originator: G.L. Britton, Spokane, Wash.
This is an easy-to-tie Chironomid pupa pattern developed by guide G.L. Britton. The fly sinks rapidly and has proved effective at Inland Northwest stillwaters. The most popular bead colors are brass, copper, gold, silver, and black. Beads are available in several sizes and weights.

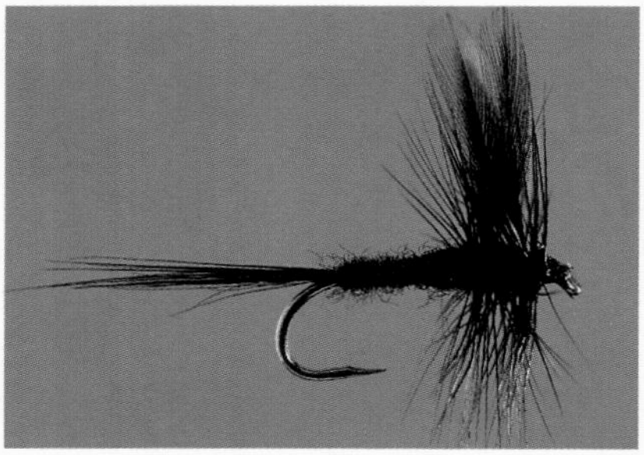

Black Midge

Hook: #16-22, Dry Fly
Thread: Black 6/0-8/0
Tail: Black hackle fibers
Body: Black dubbing
Wings: Black hackle tips
Hackle: Black

This is a good, all-around pattern for times when trout are taking dark midges. Either fur or synthetic material can be used for the dubbing. Because it doesn't absorb water, the synthetic dubbing floats longer. Black tying thread can be used for the body. All-black patterns are difficult to see under some light conditions. However, they are visible when light is reflected from the water.

Brassie

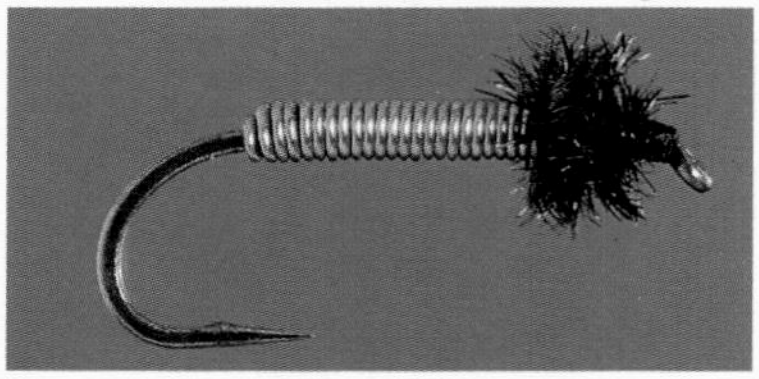

Hook: #10-22, Wet Fly, 2XL
Thread: Black 6/0
Body: Fine copper wire
Thorax: Peacock herl

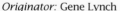

Originator: Gene Lynch
This simple pattern is one of the most effective flies wherever midges hatch. Fine copper wire creates a segmented appearance and also adds weight so the fly sinks fast. When applying peacock herl, wind thread around the herl to prevent unraveling. A variation calls for an underbody of tightly wound holographic tinsel, with the copper wire spiraled over it. The variation can represent mayfly nymphs and caddisfly pupae, as well as midge larvae.

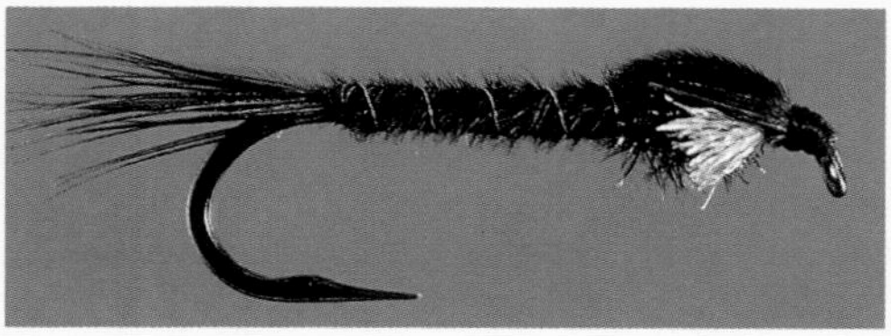

Chan's Chironomid

Hook: #10-16, Wet Fly, 2XL
Thread: Brown 6/0
Rib: Gold or silver wire
Body: Pheasant tail
Wingcase: Pheasant tail
Thorax: Peacock herl
Gills: White Antron

Originator: Brian Chan, Kamloops, B.C.
Most tiers of this popular pattern prefer short white Antron or poly fibers or guinea hen fibers for a tail. For light bodies, use light reddish brown pheasant tail and medium gold wire; for dark versions, use dark pheasant tail and silver wire. Gills are usually tied crosswise under wingcase, but many tiers prefer to tie a tuft of Antron over the hook eye. Wingcase can be brown turkey wing or raffia.

Midge Emerger
Hook: #20-22, Dry Fly
Thread: Gray or black 8/0
Tail: Brown Z-lon wisps
Body: Gray chinchilla
Rib: Gray or black thread 8/0
Wingcase: White Z-lon

Originator: Clay Findlay, Spokane, Wash.
The originator, who reputedly fishes no less than 300 days a year, created this pattern to simulate emerging Chironomids on one of his favorite slow-moving, meandering streams. The pattern has been effective everywhere midges hatch. The body should be thinly dubbed and the wingcase formed with a short clump of Z-lon.

Griffith's Gnat
Hook: #14-24, Dry Fly
Thread: Black 8/0
Hackle: Grizzly
Body: Peacock herl

Originator: George Griffith, Grayling, Mich.
This is a highly effective pattern when Chironomids are hatching. It suggests a partially hatched midge or a cluster of adult midges and is often fished in the surface film. Some tiers prefer turned-down-eye hooks for large patterns and turned-up-eye hooks for small flies. High grade grizzly hackle is wound from the hook bend to the eye of the hook.

Lady McConnell
Hook: #10-20, Dry Fly
Thread: Tan, gray, or brown
Shuck: Grizzly hackle tip
Back and Wing: Deer hair
Body: Gray polypropylene

Originator: Brian Chan, Kamloops, B.C.
Thousands of Northwest fly fishers use this emerger during Chironomid hatches. When tying the overlay, tie in a clump of deer hair at start of hook bend, bring the thread forward, tie in the body, bring the deer hair over top and tie down. The deer hair tips extend forward at about a 45-degree angle. Fish this pattern when trout switch over from feeding on pupae and begin gorging themselves on emerging insects.

Lasha's Chironomid Emerger
Hook: #12-20, Dry Fly
Thread: Black 8/0
Wing: Coastal deer hair
Rib: Silver or gold wire
Body: Fur or synthetic dubbing
Gills: White ostrich or emu

Originator: Paul Lasha
This pattern is effective when trout are taking emerging Chironomids. The color of the thread and dubbing should match the color of the hatching insects. The fine deer hair should be bleached tan or brown and tied forward over the hook eye at a 45-degree angle, suggesting an insect that's struggling out of its shuck. Lasha's pattern has proved effective at scores of lakes and reservoirs in the Northwest.

Chironomids

Palomino Midge

Hook: #16-22, Scud
Thread: Black 8/0
Abdomen: Ultra chenille
Wingcase: White Z-lon
Thorax: Black dubbing

Originator: Brett Smith

This pattern suggests emerging midges and is fished in the surface film. Use ultra thin chenille for the extended body. New Dub makes a good substitute. The most popular abdomen hues are black, red, brown, and gray. The white Z-lon is tied in at the rear of the thorax, then dubbing is used to build up the thorax. The Z-lon is then tied forward and down, extending over the eye of the hook and clipped off.

Penny Bright Midge

Hook: #10-20, Scud
Thread: Fine copper wire, use a bobbin
Rib: Fine copper wire
Body: Superfloss
Wingcase: Turkey tail
Thorax: Peacock herl
Gills: White Z-lon

Originator: Jim Shearer, Kennewick, Wash.
Wind a base of wire from near the hook eye to around the bend; leave a three-inch tag of wire. Spiral wire from bobbin forward, and attach Superfloss with three wraps of wire. Wrap Superfloss and secure at rear with three wire wraps of tag, then spiral tag forward as a rib. Attach other materials and finish fly with wire. Match Superfloss color to the natural's color, black, brown, or olive.

Red Butt Chironomid

Hook: #10-14, Wet Fly
Thread: Black 6/0
Butt: Red floss
Rib: Fine gold tinsel
Abdomen: Pheasant tail
Shellback: Pheasant tail
Thorax: Peacock herl
Gills: White ostrich herl

Originator: Brian Chan, Kamloops, B.C.
This pattern suggests emerging Chironomid larvae, or "bloodworms." The red butt simulates a hemoglobin-like respiratory fluid that allows larvae to live in deep, low-oxygen environments. Chan recommends fishing the pattern with floating line and up to 16 to 20 feet of leader. Because the larvae move extremely slowly, it's doubly important to fish the pattern dead slow. Pheasant tail fibers or synthetic brown raffia can be used for the shellback.

Serendipity

Hook: #14-22, Scud
Thread: 8/0
Body: Z-lon, twisted
Wing and Head: Deer hair tuft

The Serendipity simulates midge or caddis larvae. The thread color should match that of the body. The most popular colors are brown, olive, and red. Some tiers use V-Rib material or tightly wound Krystal Flash for the body. For a bead-head variation, don't tie in a deer hair tuft, but add a small, dubbed thorax behind the bead. This pattern was developed for fishing Montana streams, and now is one of the most popular patterns in the West.

Skinny Minnie

Hook: #8-16, Dry Fly, 2XL
Thread: Olive 6/0
Rib: Gold wire
Body: Fine peacock herl
Hackle: Pheasant or partridge

Originator: Don Carlson, Spokane, Wash.

This simple pattern, created in 1968, suggests hatching insects. The pattern, nearly always fished in the surface film, simulates an insect emerging into an adult. Wind poor quality herl, twisted around tying thread, to create a slender body. For the hackle, tie one or two turns of either blue-gray pheasant rump or Hungarian partridge.

Swannundaze Chironomid

Hook: #10-16, Wet Fly, 2XL
Thread: Black 6/0
Body: Swannundaze or V-Rib
Thorax: Peacock herl
Gills: White Antron fibers

Popularized by Seattle-area fly fishers, the Swannundaze Chironomid is one of the most effective Chironomid pupa patterns in the Northwest. Swannundaze and V-Rib plastic, oval on one side and flat on the other, are available in various widths and colors. The most important colors, in order of popularity, are black, brown, green and red. Tying options include flattened wire under the Swannundaze for weight, a tail of white Antron fibers, and a rib of gold or silver wire.

YDC

Hook: #6-16, 2XL
Thread: Black 6/0-8/0
Rib: White thread
Body: Black poly or Antron yarn
Overlay: Pheasant rump or turkey
Thorax: White ostrich herl
Hackle: Brown hackle wisps

Originator: Wayne Yoshida, Vancouver, B.C.

The initials stand for Yoshida's Delectable Chironomid. The pattern, created in the 1970s, is still popular, especially in British Columbia. Vary the body color to match the pupae that are hatching. The hackle is optional; most tiers omit it. Some fly fishers tie a few wisps of white Antron for a tail.

Caddisflies

Adults

Pharate Adult

Larvae

addisflies are among the most abundant (7,000 species worldwide) and widespread families of aquatic insects. They are often the first preference for trout. Yet, in years past not many anglers used caddisfly patterns. Before the late 1970s, lack of information and published misinformation misled and frustrated many fly anglers. Misinformed fly anglers often used the wrong flies in the wrong places at the wrong times and with the wrong techniques.

This information void ended in the late 1970s and early 1980s when Larry Solomon and Eric Leiser wrote *The Caddis and the Angler* and Gary LaFontaine authored *Caddisflies*. LaFontaine's book is a definitive work, based on years of research. It added tremendously to the fly-fishing world's knowledge about caddisflies. His studies also led to the development of new caddisfly patterns and fishing techniques. *Caddisflies* is recommended to any serious fly angler who wants to understand these ubiquitous insects.

The name of the caddisfly order "Trichoptera" is derived from the Greek *trichos* (hair) and *pteron* (wing) which refers to the dense mat of microscopic hairs covering the wings of the adult. The wings are normally held over the back in a distinctive tent shape. Adult caddisflies are often referred to as sedges.

In North America, more than 1,200 species of caddisflies range in size from minute microcaddis 1/8 to 1/4 inches long (hook sizes 24 and 22) to giants 1 1/4 to 1 1/2 inches long (hook sizes 4 or 2). Fortunately, detailed knowledge of 1,200 species isn't necessary to fish with caddisfly patterns successfully. The examination of caddis larvae on stream beds and flying adult sedges is often the easiest way to determine which patterns will be productive. Caddisflies typically have a one-year life cycle: egg-larva-pupa-adult, and inhabit all types of still and moving water.

Larva

Entomologists classify caddisfly families according to the habitat and living habits of the larvae. Free-living larvae like the green sedge (genus *Rhyacophila*) crawl over riffle-area rocks in cool streams. Other larvae build nets of various styles and shapes to trap food and come out of their shelters only to tend their nets. Finally, there are several families of case builders that construct fixed or mobile homes of rocks or twigs. Trout feed on both free-living and cased larvae.

Pupa

Eventually, the larva seals itself into a protective chamber and undergoes a two- to three-week metamorphosis into an adult. The insect then cuts its way out of the pupal chamber and inflates its pupal covering with gas to help it rise to the surface. Scientists call this form a pharate adult, which comes from the Greek word *pharos*, meaning garment. The pharate adult is a mature adult within its pupal sheath. Of importance to fly anglers is that in moving water this stage of the insect drifts with the current, and some genera, such as the very common spotted sedge, remain in their sheath near the bottom of the stream for a considerable distance. Trout take advantage of this helpless stage as the pharate adult begins its trip to the surface.

The speed of the insects' movement toward the surface varies with different species, but is not the "rocket-like" rise claimed in early literature. As the pharate adult rises, light reflects through the gas-inflated pupal covering and causes a mirror-like sparkle that trout key on. Trout sometimes follow the rising pharate adult and strike when it pauses at the surface.

Lake species follow the same pattern of leaving the pupal chamber, inflating the pupal covering, and rising to the surface. However, the upward migration is a series of active swimming motions and short rest periods.

Caddisflies

Many fly casters still mistakenly call the pharate adult a pupa, so you will find "pupa" in the current literature and in the patterns for several flies listed here.

Adult

At the surface, there is sometimes a short delay before the pupal covering splits and the adult struggles free and flies off to shoreline vegetation. Feeding trout take advantage of this short delay.

Some newly emerged lake and stream species don't fly away immediately. The traveling sedges, some over one inch long, of British Columbia and elsewhere, scurry across the surface before becoming airborne. Other caddisflies in both lakes and streams move in spirals before flying off. These active adults create a disturbance that attracts the attention of nearby trout.

After mating, some females drop their eggs into the water from a safe height, and others dip to the water's surface to wash off their eggs. But several species lay their eggs underwater, and the females carry bubbles of air with them as they descend to lay their eggs. Trout key on the mirror-like reflection of the bubbles and take many females.

Patterns and Angling Tactics

Streams and Caddisfly Larvae

Larvae near the stream bottom are best imitated with patterns like the Green Rock Worm, Cactus Caddis or a Sparkle Cased Caddis. Colors and sizes of cased caddisflies vary from stream to stream and even from one water flow to another (slow, medium, to fast) within a stream. If you don't know the patterns the locals use, look for naturals in the different types of water. An angler should carry a variety of imitations when fishing unfamiliar waters. If nothing matches, break out the tying kit.

Look for trout feeding on larvae in boulder runs, riffles, and below riffles where trout might wait for drifting Sparkle Cased Caddis. Cast a weighted pattern upstream; let it sink and drift downstream with the current like a dislodged natural. Use up-stream mends to keep a belly from forming in the line and dragging the fly downstream too fast. A foam float or yarn strike indicator will help control the depth of your fly, and any strange movement of the indicator (stopping, moving sideways, or plunging underwater) can mean you have a strike. A guideline for most runs or holes is to set the fly-to-indicator distance at about twice the water depth.

In a stream, some of the largest fish hide in deep holes where the surface is fast and fly anglers or other predators can't see them. Use a heavy fly like a weighted Sparkle Cased Caddis, two heavy split shot about a foot from the fly, and a big strike indicator. With such a setup, set the strike-indicator-to-fly distance equal to the water depth being fished. Cast it into the head of a deep hole and watch the indicator. If it moves strangely at all, strike.

The Stream Hatch

Hours before a hatch peaks, some caddis begin cutting out of their pupal chambers and drifting near the bottom. Fish feed on these early adults. Cast a weighted version of the Emergent Sparkle Caddis Pupa upstream or up-and-across and fish with a dead-drift, nymph style. Air trapped by the Antron shuck and overbody reflects light as the natural does when it inflates its pupal sheath. As you fish the fly, occasionally tighten the line and quickly follow with a mend that drops the fly back into a dead-drift.

When fish start taking naturals just under the surface, it's time to switch to emerger fly patterns. Cast an Emergent Sparkle Caddis Pupa upstream, let it sink and then tighten the fly line, making the fly swing upward and drift just under the surface. To simulate caddisflies that are struggling to break through the surface, dead-drift an X-Caddis or Midway Caddis. An occasional twitch of the fly usually improves your success rate.

Another extremely effective technique is the wet-fly swing using Britton I and II flies in riffles and runs or any soft hackle pattern in slower water. Cast quartering downstream, let the fly drift downstream a bit and then tighten the line to make the fly move across the current. *(See caddisfly hatch chart on page 128.)*

Dry–fly Stream Fishing

Floating patterns are important at the right time. Adults can live for weeks or even months after emerging, but they return to the water to drink and lay eggs. Drift an Elk Hair Caddis, Goddard Caddis, or X-Caddis along undercut banks and low-hanging vegetation. The X-Caddis is good when there are spent females on the surface.

The evening rise can be the best time to fish dry-fly caddis imitations. At times, flying caddis on Western streams are so thick there is a noticeable dimming of the already subdued evening light. Fish become extremely active under these conditions and take hatching caddis or egg-laying females aggressively. Use an Elk Hair Caddis or Goddard Caddis in any color, including black, and keep fishing into the darkness when a splash where your fly should be is the only indication of a strike. The wet-fly swing mentioned above is also effective during the evening rise.

Lake Fishing During Emergence

Use a floating line and a leader long enough to reach the bottom. Be alert for a take as a fly like the Traveling Sedge Pupa is sinking. Let it rest on the bottom and then make two or three quick hand-twist retrieves and pause. Then two more quick hand twists and a pause. Repeat this sequence until you have a fish on or the fly is at the surface.

Dry Flies In Lakes

Dry-fly action starts when the adults reach the surface and begin leaving the pupal covering. Many species hatch during the day, and often there's more than one species on the water. Watch the naturals and try to imitate their actions with an Elk Hair Caddis or Slow Water Caddis. If fish ignore your fly, a twitch will attract their attention.

During a traveling sedge hatch, strip large flies, like a Mikulak's Sedge or Goddard Caddis, across the surface. Be sure the excess fly line is free to rip through the guides when the hooked fish makes its first run.

Wind is a fact of life during a caddisfly hatch. Tom Thumb and Black Foam Caddis are super floaters in all conditions. Cast cross-wind or slightly downwind and let the fly blow across the surface. Most of the time the fly is not visible, so watch for a splash past the end of the fly line, then set the hook.

Caddisflies

Caddisfly Larvae and Pupae

Cactus Caddis
Hook: #8-20, Wet Fly, 2-3XL
Thread: Black 6/0
Underbody: Crystal Chenille
Overbody: Hare's ear dubbing
Larva Body: Green dubbing
Legs: Brown partridge
Head: Brown or black dubbing

Originator: Rene' Harrop, St. Anthony, Ida.

As pictured, this cased caddisfly variation is appropriate to streams having light-colored gravel bottoms. Examine local caddisfly cases and select the color of sparkle chenille and dubbing to match. The dubbed overbody may be so thin that it is barely seen or so thick that it nearly hides the chenille. Tie heavily weighted.

Colorado Caddis
Hook: #10-20, Scud
Thread: Yellow or black 6/0
Shellback: Goose wing quill
Body: Pale yellow dubbing
Hackle: Black hen hackle
Head: Black thread, large

Originator: Bob Good, Denver, Colo.

This is a variation of the original. Larger versions have long been a Colorado favorite for fishing in riffles, deep holes, and slow water. Despite its name, it resembles a caddisfly poorly, but takes fish. Wrap hackle as a collar then pull shellback forward through it. Antennae of black hackle fibers are optional. Body may be wool, rabbit or poly in colors yellow to light green.

Doc Spratley
Hook: #8-10, Wet Fly, 2-3XL
Thread: Black 3/0
Tail: Grizzly hackle fibers
Rib: Silver oval tinsel
Body: Black wool
Hackle: Grizzly
Wing: Pheasant tail
Head: Peacock herl

Originator: Dick Prankard, Mount Vernon, Wash.

This 1949 pattern, named after the late Dr. Donald A. Spratley of Mount Vernon, Wash., is still one of the most effective wet-fly patterns in British Columbia. In waters with good traveling sedge hatches many anglers prefer a green body. Another variation is tied with a brown body, gold rib and brown hackle. Some anglers like a slender body, and others a full abdomen. Tie the hackle down into a beard, as shown.

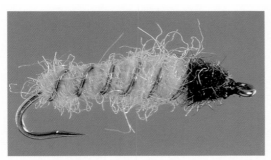

Green Rock Worm

Hook: #8-20, Wet Fly, 2-3XL
Thread: Black 6/0, 8/0
Rib: Copper wire
Abdomen: Green sparkle dubbing
Head: Black Hare-Tron

The free-living *Rhyacophila* caddisfly doesn't build a protective case and is abundant in fast-current streams of the West. This pattern is a combination of those inspired by Polly Rosborough, Randall Kaufmann, and Gary Borger. It is usually fished dead-drift near bottom. Variations include a rib of green wire, pheasant tail barbs as a beard, peacock herl for the head, and dubbed abdomen colors from light green to bright green.

Sparkle Cased Caddis

Hook: #8, Wet Fly, 2-3XL
Head: Black brass bead
Thread: Black 3/0
Underbody: Variegated
  chenille
Overbody: Hare's ear dubbing
Body: Yellow or cream dub-
  bing

Originator: G.L. Britton,
Spokane, Wash.

In northern Idaho, case-building caddisflies include garnet chips in their protective housings. The red color and flash is simulated with red and black variegated plastic chenille or red Krystal Flash cut in 3/16-inch lengths. Green Krystal Flash pieces can be added to match naturals in other areas. The heavy, 3/16-inch, black bead is an excellent imitation of the natural's head and is a good non-lead weight.

Traveling Sedge Pupa

Hook: #10, Dry Fly, 2-3XL
Thread: Olive 6/0
Rib: Bright green wire
Body: Golden olive yarn
Legs: Olive dyed partridge
Head Rib: Fine silver wire
Head: Peacock herl

Originator: Frank Slak, Spokane, Wash. Legs are a prominent feature, and are used as oars to swim upward in the water column. Montana and British Columbia sedge hatches begin in June. Use a floating line with long leader, cast, and let the fly reach bottom. Make three quick hand twists, pause, then two hand twists, pause, and continue until fly is at the surface. Dubbed bodies, tinsel ribs, and olive-green colors are options. Many tiers weight this pattern.

Caddisflies *(vertical, left margin)*

Caddisfly Emergers

Britton I and II

Hook: #12-16, Scud
Thread: Yellow 6/0
Body: I - Yellow floss
   II - Pink floss
Hackle: I - Grizzly
   II - Ginger

Originator: Les Britton, Moscow, Ida.
These two flies were developed for use on the Cache La Poudre River in Colorado around 1945. Even though they are tied with dry-fly hackle, they are fished like soft-hackled wet flies in riffles and runs. Usually fished in dropper fashion as follows: 4X tippet (3X in early summer) to the Britton II (pink, shown), then 15 inches 5X tippet to the Britton I (yellow) point fly.

CDC Caddis Emerger

Hook: #16-18, Scud
Thread: Brown 8/0
Rib: Copper wire
Abdomen: Brown dubbing
Wing: Brown CDC and hen feathers
Legs: Brown saddle fibers
Thorax: Brown fine dubbing

Originator: Arnie Gidlow, Cascade, Mont.
This rough-looking pattern was developed in 1993 to fish spring creeks and tailwaters for highly selective trout. Fish it with a dead-drift in or just under the surface film. Neither the fly nor leader are weighted; don't dress the fly. CDC (Cul de Canard) feathers are sandwiched between two vertically tied hen saddle feathers.

Emergent Sparkle Caddis Pupa

Hook: #12-20, Dry Fly
Thread: Green 6/0
Shuck: Antron
Overbody: Pale green Antron
Underbody: Green to brown dubbing
Wing: Light deer hair
Head: Brown dubbing

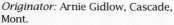

Originator: Gary LaFontaine, Deer Lodge, Mont.
The reflective qualities of Antron simulate the gas bubbles seen around emerging caddis pupae. Fish feed on emergent forms before taking surface adults. The pattern can also be used to imitate other food sources in the surface film or backwater foam lines. Underbody is a mixture of fur and Antron loosely dubbed, and the tail is a few strands of green, rust, or gold Antron. Dub the head in any contrasting color.

Foam Black Caddis

Hook: #4-8, Dry Fly, 2XL
Thread: Black 3/0
Tail: Deer hair
Body: Black closed cell foam
Underwing: Dark deer hair
Overwing: Light deer hair

Originator: Al Cunningham, Spokane, Wash.
Originally developed in 1994 for use on Canadian lakes, it has hooked many fish under strong wind conditions. The wrapped closed-cell foam body keeps it floating in heavy waves. Cast the fly 45 degrees downwind, let the wind move it and occasionally twitch the fly with a 3- to 6-inch strip. It attracts fish even when there is no hatch in progress. Black or grizzly hackle and white calf tail wings are options.

Midway Caddis

Hook: #16, Scud
Thread: Brown Uni-thread 8/0
Shuck: Caddis orange Z-lon
Wing: Deer hair
Abdomen: Hare's mask dubbing
Thorax: Darker dubbing

Originator: Harry Mayo, West Yellowstone, Mont.
Wing position is "midway" down the body. This fly should be fished upstream, dead-drift on a leader greased to about a foot from fly. Soak the fly so it drifts just below the surface. It imitates a stillborn cripple or, possibly, a drowned adult. Stack deer hair, stand it up and wrap thread around base to hold fibers together. Wood duck for legs is optional.

Scintillator Caddis

Hook: #14-16, Dry Fly
Thread: Green 8/0
Abdomen: Green dubbing
Gas Bubble: 3 x 6 mm bead
Wing and Legs: Partridge
Head: Gray ostrich

Originator: Kenn Ligas, Belgrade, Mont.
This pattern utilizes commercially available football-shaped, pearlescent plastic beads to mimic bubbles seen around emerging caddis. Dub abdomen then dub thin underbody, whip finish, clip thread, slide crystal bead over the hook eye, and underbody. Finish wing, legs and head. Fish dead-drift or downstream and across. Variations: lime to bright green, black, and sepia for abdomen and brown or light gray ostrich (or dubbing) for head. Wide gape, straight eye hooks are recommended.

Spring Creek Caddis Pupa

Hook: #14-22, Scud
Thread: Brown 6/0
Overbody: White organza
Body: Rust goose biot
Legs: Partridge fibers
Thorax: Dubbing to match body
Antennae: Partridge fibers

Originator: Arnie Gidlow, Cascade, Mont. Sparkle organza is wedding veil material available in various colors in fly shops and fabric stores. Use fibers pulled from the edge of a one-inch square of organza for the over-body. It mimics the bubble-like qualities of a hatching caddis. Body and thorax variations include brown, gray, and light olive. In micropattern sizes (18-22), it is a great spring creek and stillwater fly. Also called Organza Caddis Pupa.

Tom Thumb

Hook: #6-14, Dry Fly, 2XL
Thread: Black 3/0
Tail: Deer body hair
Body and Wing: Deer hair

The forward wing looks like a hatching caddisfly and rough lake waves can't sink it. Body, overlay, and wing are tied from the same bundle of deer body hair. Tie it in by the butt, bring overlay

forward either surrounding the hook or only on top half, secure and let wings point forward. Some tiers wrap red or yellow floss on body before bringing overlay forward. Tie many because fish usually tear them apart.

X-Caddis

Hook: #14-18, Dry Fly
Thread: Tan or olive 6/0
Shuck: Amber gold Z-lon
Body: Tan or olive dubbing
Wing: Deer hair

Originator: Craig Mathews, West Yellowstone, Mont. Developed about 1980 for Rocky Mountain streams, this all-season fly is fished in the surface film by greas-ing only the wing. Fish that refuse other patterns will take this low-profile fly. Fish continue to take this fly when only three or four

hairs are left in the wing. Body and shuck colors should match natural's. Beaver dubbing works well and the Z-lon shuck should be crinkled.

Caddisfly Adult

Elk Hair Caddis

Hook: #6-20, Dry Fly
Thread: Tan 6/0
Rib: Gold wire, fine
Body: Rabbit or poly dubbing
Hackle: Brown palmered
Wing: Elk body hair

Originator: Al Troth, Dillon, Mont.
This fly is a standard adult caddisfly pattern for many anglers. It floats well in almost any water. Tying it is easy: tie on wire, dub body forward, tie on hackle and palmer it rearward. Lock in hackle with gold wire and spiral wire forward. Attach wing and trim butts even with hook's eye. Body color and hackle to match the natural's include olive, tan, brown, and black.

Goddard Caddis

Hook: #10-16, Dry Fly
Thread: Tan 6/0
Body: Tan deer
Hackle: Brown
Antennae: Brown hackle stem

Originators: John Goddard and Cliff Henry

An excellent rough-water pattern developed in early 1970s. Spun and trimmed deer or caribou hair keeps it floating in almost any type of water conditions. Large sizes are useful during traveling sedge hatches in British Columbia lakes. Variations may be any tan or brown color of the tier's choice. In all black it is an excellent nighttime pattern on the Madison or other turbulent rivers.

Mikulak's Sedge

Hook: #8-12, Dry Fly, 3XL
Thread: Olive green 3/0
Tail and Wings: Elk hair
Body: Green or brown dubbing
Hackle: Brown or dun

Originator: Arthur "Mitch" Mikulak, Calgary, Alberta
Older fly books call this fly Mitch's Sedge, but the preferred name according to B.C. fly fishers is Mikulak's Sedge. When large caddisflies are hatching this fly is a must. Three bundles of elk hair are used: one for tail, one about mid-shank, and third in front. Keep wings in a tapered caddisfly shape. Ends of the front bundle are clipped for the head.

Parachute Caddis

Hook: #12-18, Dry Fly
Thread: Tan 8/0
Abdomen: Tan poly
Hackle: Brown
Wing: Light elk hair

Originator: Jan Sadlo, Spokane, Wash.
Jan developed a unique way of wrapping his parachute hackle. Using a tight dubbing loop, wrap a tapered body and secure (but don't trim the loop). Attach hackle and stacked elk hair. Continue wrapping dubbing loop forward to front of body. Wind hackle around base of wing and butts. Variations: Olive or yellow body with brown hackle, gray body with grizzly hackle, all black and all cream.

Slow Water Caddis

Hook: #12-22, Dry Fly
Thread: Brown 8/0
Body: Brown dubbing
Hackle: Brown
Underwing: Brown deer hair
Wing: Brown turkey biot

Originator: Rene' Harrop, St. Anthony, Ida.
This pattern was originally tied with hackle tip wings. In the early 1990s, Rene' Harrop started working with biot wings and they proved to be very effective. Tie biots in by their tips, and bend the tips up to simulate eyes or a small head. Trim rear of biots to look like caddisfly wings. Variations are black, gray, ginger and any other color to match the hatch. Brown hackle fibers for antennae are optional.

Spring Creek Caddis

Hook: #16-18, Scud
Thread: Brown 6/0
Abdomen: Brown elk hock
Wing: Brown fly film
Antennae: Microfibbets
Legs: Wood duck or mallard
Thorax: Dark brown dubbing

Originator: Arnie Gidlow, Cascade, Mont.
This is an ideal spring creek and tailwater fly when fished dead-drift or skittered across surface. Abdomen is tied extended-body style and cut square at rear. Place wing over body with notch at end of extended body. A CDC feather can be added as an overwing. Tie legs facing forward. Dub thin noodle, wrap behind and in front of fibers to make them face rearward. Also called Extended Body Caddis.

Adults

Nymphs

Damselflies and Dragonflies

Adult

Nymph

Damselflies and dragonflies are two important stillwater food sources. Both have incomplete metamorphosis life cycles with egg, nymph, and adult stages.

The nymphs of both pass through several stages of molting before they mature. Then when water temperatures rise above 60 degrees, they migrate toward shore and climb out on reeds, protruding logs, or rocks. These migrations can initiate feeding frenzies by fish. Once out of the water, the nymph splits its exoskeleton and the adult emerges. Damselfly adults are sometimes vulnerable to fish, but dragonfly adults usually aren't because they're such strong fliers. However, both damselfly and dragonfly females become vulnerable when they lay eggs.

Damselflies

Damselflies are common throughout the Northwest. They're most often found in shallow, weedy stillwaters and are less prevalent in deep lakes and moving water. Most damselflies have a one-year life cycle.

Damselflies and Dragonflies

Damselfly nymphs have slim, segmented bodies up to 1 1/2 inches in length, and two or three leaf-like gills. Like chameleons, their color matches that of their background. Damselfly nymph colors range from light olive to dark olive, and from tan to reddish brown, and the nymphs are always lighter on the underside. In some marl-bottom lakes, they have very pale coloring. They're predators, and when they're feeding, they climb over submerged vegetation or wait in hiding for prey to pass.

Mature damselfly nymphs swim to the surface and migrate to shore just under the surface film. Large migrations occur from May in low-elevation lakes to late June in high, cooler waters. They usually begin about mid–morning and continue into late morning or early afternoon. Smaller migrations occur through the summer months. Some species that migrate early in the summer have two or more broods per year, and other species mature just once in August or September.

The nymphs' sculling movements are quite pronounced, but their forward progress is fairly slow. They are also slow when climbing out on reeds to hatch. They're easy targets, and trout feed on them, sometimes selectively.

Damselfly adult vulnerability must be considered at three stages of development. First, tenerals (immature adults) hang onto the hatching surfaces for some time to expand and dry their wings after leaving the nymphal exoskeleton. When they fly, a wind gust can blow these weak fliers into the water. Second, adults often land on floating weeds and debris or fly low over the water. Third, late in the season when other major hatches are over, fish become interested in egg-laying damselfly females.

Damselfly Patterns and Angling Tactics

Because large numbers of trout are attracted to nymphs swimming near the surface during a migration, the fishing can be fantastic. But this is a small part of damselfly-fishing.

Before and After Migrations

Drag a Bead Head Damsel, Damselfly Nymph, Extended Body Damsel, Pheasant Tail Six Pack or Superfly along the edges of weed beds or lake-bottom debris, using a sink-tip or full-sinking line.

You must attempt to imitate the natural: Size, color, silhouette, and movement are all important. Marabou dressings imitate the action of a swimming nymph when fished with a hand twist or "strip/tease" retrieve. For a "strip/tease" retrieve, the line is stripped a foot in three to four seconds while the rod tip is vibrated up and down or side to side. This causes the fly to both move and twitch.

During Migration

Since nymphs usually migrate toward shore, retrieve your fly in that direction if at all possible. However, any object extending above the surface, such as a stump or reed, will attract migrating nymphs, so look for other patterns of moving nymphs.

Most fish key on nymphs just under the surface film, so your fly should be in that zone. A floating line, greased leader, light-wire-hook pattern, DF Damsel or Back Pack Damsel, and slow hand–twist retrieve will keep the fly close to the surface. Many fish rush to take a fly and immediately turn back to their feeding lane so violently that they snap even heavy tippets. To avoid this, let the rod absorb the shock by pointing it to one side so there is a 90 degree angle between it and the fly line.

Teneral (Immature Adult)

There are always a few fish that look for hatching nymphs or immature adults. They are thought to jump against reeds or cattails to grab or knock off tenerals that aren't ready for flight. There are two approaches to catch these fish. Use a damselfly nymph and cast it next to the reeds, let it sink for a few seconds, and then strip it in. Or cast a tan to dirty-olive adult damselfly pattern, like the Braided Butt Adult Damsel, near the reeds and twitch it occasionally.

Adult

Some books say that adult damselfly imitations are of no value, but Inland Northwest anglers have discovered otherwise. Blue and tan are the most common colors. When fish are jumping to grab hovering or low-flying adults, throw a Foam Adult Damsel or Braided Butt Adult Damsel into the rise ring, let it sit quietly for 3 to 5 seconds and then wiggle the rod tip a little. When damsels are laying their eggs, fish a floating female imitation (olives, tans, browns, pale yellow) with the same sit-then-twitch technique.

Dragonflies

Dragonflies are the bully boys of insects; adults have wingspans measuring up to five inches. Dragonfly nymphs live two to three years, making them an important source of food year-round, especially in the winter when many other aquatic insects are too small to be seen.

The nymphs are powerfully built. Some species are short and stocky, less than an inch long, while others are long and thick, up to 2 1/2 inches long. All dragonfly nymphs have bulbous abdomens and an hourglass shape. Their gills are inside the abdomen and they draw water into the rectal chamber for respiration. They can expel this water forcefully, driving themselves forward in quick, jet-propelled spurts. Their colors range from olive-gray to muddy brown, giving the nymphs good camouflage in their habitat of mud and decaying vegetation. Some of the nymphs prowl the bottom in search of prey, while others burrow into lake bottoms and wait for prey with only their eyes and the tip of their abdomens showing.

Migrating nymphs usually crawl along the bottom toward shore and wait in shallows before climbing out of the water after dark.

Dragonfly Patterns and Angling Tactics

Dragonfly nymph imitations can be effective any time of year. If you're fishing when the nymphs are not migrating, sink an imitation deep, either near the bottom or just above weed beds. Count the seconds it takes for the line to reach bottom or a weed bed. Then shorten the sink time a few seconds and retrieve. Use a rapid, start-stop retrieve, 5 to 10 inches per pull, to simulate the jet-propelled action of the natural. To simulate a burrowing species, let the fly sink to the bottom, then kick up a little mud during the retrieve. Fish sometimes feed on migrating nymphs or those waiting near shore to leave the water.

Since dragonfly nymphs live up to three years, several different sizes are present at any time. Therefore, imitations should range from size 4 (6X long) down to size 12 (2X long). Carey Special, Ed Wolf's Dragonfly Nymph, Gomphus and other patterns given here catch fish for Northwest anglers.

Damselflies and Dragonflies

Damselfly Nymphs

Bead Head Damsel
Hook: #12, Wet Fly
Head: Black bead
Thread: Olive 6/0
Rib: Gold wire
Body: Olive dubbing
Wingcase: Pheasant hackle
Legs and Tail: Pheasant hackle

Originator: Ben Wolen, Cheney, Wash.

Tied sparse, this fly is very effective. It is probably taken as a Chironomid pupa imitation. Yellow-dyed pheasant produces an olive color that works extremely well to match insects in the Northwest. The tail, thorax, wingcase, and legs are all tied with fibers from pheasant back feathers, as shown. Fish this fly deep in weeds where damselfly nymphs crawl over aquatic plants searching for prey. Move the fly slowly with a hand-twist retrieve.

Damselfly Nymph
Hook: #8-14, Wet Fly, 2XL
Thread: Olive 6/0
Tail: Olive marabou
Body: Olive hare's mask
Wingcase: Turkey tail fibers
Head and Thorax: Hare's mask

This generic pattern fills the bill for much damselfly nymph fishing. Marabou gives the undulating motion characteristic of damselfly nymphs as they move. Before and after nymph migrations, fish around weeds with sink-tip or slow-sinking lines, and vary the retrieve. Like chameleons, nymphs often take on the coloring of their surroundings; hence materials in shades of olive, green, tan, and brown are needed to match the color of naturals.

Extended Body Damsel
Hook: #14, Scud
Thread: Olive or brown 6/0
Tail: Olive marabou
Extended Body: Ultra Chenille
Wingcase: Pheasant tail fibers
Thorax: Olive Antron, dubbed
Eyes: Burned monofilament

Originator: Ed Burk, Visalia, Calif.
This variation of the Bug-Eyed Damsel by John Jones of Spokane, Wash., was inspired by a catalog picture. Assemble the tail and extended body on a needle or thin wire held in vise, slip it off the wire, trim excess marabou and Ultra Chenille, and put a drop of Super Glue on thread. Expose thread core of extended body before tying onto hook to allow free movement. Also tied tan to brown.

Pheasant Tail Six Pack

Hook: #8-10, Wet Fly, 2-4XL
Thread: Tan or olive 6/0
Rib: Gold wire, medium
Tail and Body: Pheasant tail feather
Hackle: Pheasant rump feather

Originator: Carl Haufler, Linwood, Wash.

This is one of the more popular wet flies in the Northwest. The original 1965 Six Pack required a body of long-hackled, pheasant-rump feathers. A pheasant's skin has few suitable feathers, but Everett Caryl of Spokane, Washington, found that yellow-dyed pheasant-tail fibers are a good substitute that match the coloration of damselflies. His varia-

tion is listed and provides an excellent nymph imitation, especially when fished deep around weeds.

Superfly

Hook: #12-14, Dry Fly or Scud
Weight: 3-4 wraps near bend
Thread: Olive 3/0
Tail and Body: Olive marabou
Wingcase: Olive poly yarn
Legs: Partridge body feather
Thorax and Head: Fur mix dubbing

Originator: Phil Roth, Ketchum, Ida.

George Cook of Seattle, Washington, helped popularize this pattern in the Northwest. To use it in stillwater on calm days, grease the front part of the fly and fish it slowly over shallow weed beds. Also, fish it with sinking lines and four-inch retrieves. Variations include all black and all claret. Dubbing mix is muskrat with guard hairs; brown, olive and green beaver or rabbit plus olive marabou strands. Weight with lead-free wire.

Backpack Damsel Nymph

Hook: #8-14, Dry Fly, 2XL
Thread: Olive 6/0
Eyes: Burned monofilament
Floatation: White or gray foam
Tail and Body: Olive marabou

Originator: Robert Bates, Spokane, Wash.

The center-mounted closed-cell foam keeps this fly floating in the surface film like a migrating natural. Sink the leader, and the fly will remain on top. On very windy days a floating nymph will stay near the surface regardless of wave action. Marabou from tail is twisted on thread and wrapped for body. If you tie this bug without the foam you'll get a DF Damsel, a nice subsurface fly. Use light wire hooks and a greased leader.

Damselflies and Dragonflies

Damselfly Adults

Braided Butt Adult Damsel

Hook: #10-12, Dry Fly
Thread: Olive 6/0
Abdomen: Olive braided mono
Post and Wingcase: Poly yarn
Thorax: Olive dubbing
Hackle: Blue dun

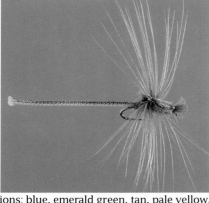

Co-originators: Bob Pelzl and Gary Borger (N.M. and Wis.)
The idea of using a braided monofilament abdomen came from New Zealand. Combined with a parachute hackle it created an excellent drowned adult damselfly. Cast near rising fish and let it sit; if nothing happens jiggle it a bit. Dye abdomen with waterproof marking pens to match colors of naturals. Variations: blue, emerald green, tan, pale yellow, and red. Burned monofilament eyes are optional.

Foam Adult Damsel

Hook: #14, Dry Fly
Thread: Black 6/0
Body: Blue braided mono
Eyes: Burned monofilament
Wingcase: Blue foam
Thorax: Blue dubbing
Wings: White, Sea Fiber

Originator: Ron Brown, Livingston, Mont.
Closed-cell foam, 1/16-inch thick and 3/16-inch wide, adds floatability, and the swept-back wings make the fly look like a spent or drowned natural. If fish are jumping for hovering adults, cast fly into the ring of the rise. If nothing happens, a wiggle like that of a weakly struggling damselfly usually attracts attention. This is an all-summer pattern which can also be tied tan to olive-green to simulate the female adult.

Dragonfly Nymphs

Butler's Bug

Hook: #4-8, Wet Fly, 3-6XL
Thread: Black 6/0
Tail: Deer hair
Abdomen: Dubbed fur
Rib: Gold or copper wire
Thorax: Dubbed fur
Shellback: Pheasant tail
Head: Peacock herl

Originator: Glen Butler, Vancouver, B.C.
This pattern for large dragonfly nymphs is effective in shades of green to tan to black. Legs are formed by tying an overhand knot one inch from fiber tips. For eyes and head, lash the pheasant tail fibers at right angles to the hook, then overwrap with peacock herl. Use 10 to 12 fibers for the legs and 5 to 10 fibers for the eyes. Buoyant deer hair from the tail tied as an underbody helps keep the fly above the lake bottom.

Carey Special

Hook: #4-12, Wet Fly, 2-3XL
Thread: Black 3/0
Tail: Pheasant rump fibers
Body: Peacock herl
Rib: Gold or silver tinsel
Hackle: Pheasant rump feather

Originator: Col. Carey, Quesnel, B.C.
This is a top-selling fly in Northwest sports shops. The 1925 original, "Monkey-Faced Louise," was supposed to imitate an emerging sedge, but it is now considered an excellent dragonfly nymph pattern when tied in brown or olive. Its early success on Kamloops, B.C. lakes soon spread throughout the Northwest. The tail may be scarlet hackle fibers and the body may be wool or chenille of any color.

Chickabou Dragon

Hook: #4-10, Wet Fly, 3-4XL
Thread: Olive 6/0
Body and Tail: Olive Chickabou
Rib: Copper wire
Hackle: Olive grizzly, soft
Wingcase: Goose wing section
Eyes: Melted mono
Head: Olive Chickabou dubbed

Originator: Henry Hoffman, Warrenton, Ore.
Henry Hoffman, developer of Hoffman Hackle, found that the soft marabou on the base of flank and belly hackles can be wrapped on hooks, forming soft marabou flies which can be trimmed to desired shape. He discards the heavy quill section. Patches of these feathers are sold under the trade name of Chickabou, or simply as hen web feathers. Rib and wingcase are optional. Weight heavily.

Draper Dragon

Hook: #6, Partridge Draper
Thread: Olive 6/0
Eyes: Black medium mono
Body: Brown olive dubbing
Legs: Pheasant tail fibers
Wingcase: Pheasant rump
Head: Brown olive dubbing

Originator: John Newbury, Chewelah, Wash.
The Draper hook H3ST has two shanks that are welded at the front and rear. It creates the flat silhouette of a dragonfly nymph without having to mash lead or use other means of making a flat body. Don't pull thread too tightly or you might break the weld. Dubbed seal fur was used on the original pattern, but seal fur substitutes work well.

Damselflies and Dragonflies

Ed Wolfe's Dragonfly Nymph

Hook: #4-12, Wet Fly, 2-4XL
Thread: Black 6/0
Tail: Peacock herl
Abdomen: Dubbing over chenille
Wingcase: Pheasant, dark fibers
Legs: Pheasant back feather
Thorax: Peacock olive chenille

Originator: Ed Wolfe, Spokane, Wash.

Distinct legs, made by stripping both ends of a ringneck pheasant church window feather, are a unique feature of this dressing. Wrap body of brown to olive dubbing over peacock olive chenille, tie in wingcase and the tip end of a church window feather. Wrap thorax, pull church window feather forward over thorax, secure, separate into six legs and lacquer them. Bring wingcase forward and form head.

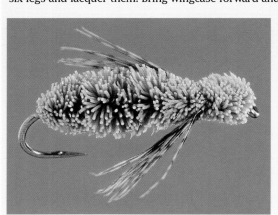

Gomphus

Hook: #8-10, Wet Fly, 2-4XL
Thread: Black 3/0
Body: Deer hair, spun
Legs: Pheasant hen tail
Head: Deer hair, spun

Originator: Jim Crawford, Polson, Mont.

The mud-dwelling *Gomphus* dragonfly nymph varies from light to dark brown in color. Deer hair may be left natural or colored with felt-tip pens. Trim hair as shown, flat on the bottom leaving a good gap at the hook point. Fish this pattern slowly and close to the bottom using a full-sinking line and short leader. The deer hair buoyancy will keep it just off the bottom.

Jolly Green Giant

Hook: #6-8, Wet Fly, 2-3XL
Thread: Olive 6/0
Tail: Pheasant rump feather
Body: Brown olive Angora goat
Hackle: Pheasant rump feather

Originator: Everett Caryl, Spokane, Wash.

The Beaverpelt Nymph is an effective dragonfly nymph imitation, but its color does not match most naturals in eastern Washington. The late Everett Caryl used brown-olive seal fur and later Angora goat for the body. The yellow-green-dyed ringneck pheasant rump feathers used for the tail and hackle on the Jolly Green Giant is an effective color combination.

Stoneflies

Adults

Nymphs

Stoneflies are among the largest and most prolific aquatic insects found in Western streams and rivers. Since trout typically feed on the largest and most abundant food source available, trout like stoneflies.

The life cycles of many stoneflies are completed in a year or less, but the larger species require two or three years to mature. Because of that, big stonefly nymphs are available as a preferred food source for trout all year long. Smaller stoneflies can be an important food source because of their large numbers at certain times.

Characteristics

Stonefly nymphs vary from 1/4 to 1 3/4 inches in length, with coloration including shades of black, brown, tan, olive-green to pale green, yellow, orange, and red. Nymphs have an elongate, segmented body with prominent antennae and two tails.

Stonefly adults are recognized by their paired translucent wings held parallel to and tight against their body. Larger stoneflies often create quite a disturbance if they fall into the water, and fly fishers imitating the larger varieties of stoneflies, such as salmonflies, try to cast the fly forcefully onto the stream surface and create a splash.

Stonefly nymphs forage along the bottom of streams and rivers for vegetation and small insects. They're usually found in highly oxygenated areas around riffles. They seek protection in rocks, but when dislodged they're available to trout. The nymphs are poor swimmers and usually crawl along the bottom. Mature nymphs migrate to shore where they crawl out of the water onto rocks and vegetation. Here they emerge from their nymphal shucks as adult flies. The life span of adults varies from a few hours up to two weeks. The

Stoneflies

adults mate and female stoneflies deposit eggs in the stream while flying or skittering over the surface. They like riffle areas for egg laying. The insect's increased activity during the hatch makes it more available to trout. In anticipation of a hatch, trout often congregate in riffles and are most easily taken just as the hatch is beginning.

Fly fishers often find riffles to be the best place to fish with stoneflies. This is partly because turbulence in riffle areas acts as protective overhead cover for fish which makes them more comfortable. Fish hold in pockets near rocks and other underwater structures, and allow the current to carry food items past their hiding place. To the benefit of anglers, the faster the current the less time a fish has to distinguish between natural food items and fly patterns. Actively feeding fish will strike at decent imitations that pass within a few feet of their holding site.

Fishing Nymph Patterns

Nymph patterns like Kauffman's Stone and the Brooks' Montana Stone are usually tied with plenty of weight. They're cast upstream so they sink to the bottom before they reach the fish. Strike indicators, attached to the line at an appropriate distance from the fly, alert the fly fisher when a fish has taken the imitation. Any deviation in the direction or speed at which the indicator is floating should trigger a strike and, hopefully, a hook up.

Upstream casts should be made 5 to 15 feet to the side of the fly fisher so that the fly can continue dead-drift past the angler downstream. As with dead-drift dry-fly fishing, nymph patterns must be presented as helpless insects caught in a current. Avoid line drag. Fish holding on the bottom aren't easily spooked by a cautious wader and long casts are unnecessary when fishing with stonefly nymphs. Fish are usually taken within 30 feet of the fly fisher.

Fishing Adult Patterns

Adult stonefly patterns are tied with abundant hair, hackle or closed-cell foam to increase buoyancy, as they are often fished in turbulent water in, or just below, riffles. High-riding, heavily hackled flies such as the Improved Sofa Pillow or Stimulator can be fished dead-drift or skittered across the surface on a downstream swing to imitate an egg-laying female.

One of the best ways to fish a stonefly hatch is by drifting downstream in a boat and casting to within a few feet of the shoreline. Large fish seek protection under overhanging vegetation. Proper line mending is essential to prevent line drag and to present the fly in a dead-drift natural form.

Different Species

The more than 450 species of stoneflies can be grouped into six major types for use by fly fishers as depicted in *Stoneflies* by Richards, Swisher and Arbora. An additional group of stoneflies active in the early spring during pre-runoff conditions is listed. The major types of stoneflies listed below are grouped into the general season in which they are most available to trout. The peak time of availability varies by location and annual fluctuations in watershed levels and water temperature. Anglers need to check with local fly shops for updated stream information before planning trips.

Winter Hatches

1. Tiny Winter Blacks, e.g. *Capnia*, midday emergence, blackish, 1/4" long, hook #14-18
2. Early Brown Stones, e.g. *Brachyptera*, late afternoon emergence, brownish, 1/2" long, hook #10-12

Spring Hatches

3. Large Yellow Stoneflies, e.g. *Skwala*, midday emergence, yellow to olive-brown, 1/2"-1" long, hook #8-12
4. Salmonflies, e.g. *Pteronarcys*, afternoon emergence, brown/black with orange thorax, 1-3/4" long, hook #2-4

Summer Hatches

5. Big Golden Stones, e.g. *Acroneuria* and *Classenia*, morning emergence, brownish yellow, 1" long, hook #6-8
6. Medium Brown Stones, e.g. *Isoperla* and *Isogenus*, midday emergence, medium brown, 1/2"-7/8" long, hook #8-12
7. Little Yellow and Green Stones, e.g. *Alloperla*, late afternoon emergence, pale yellow to olive, 1/2" long, hook #10-12

Stonefly Nymphs

Bitch Creek
Hook: #4-12, Wet Fly, 2-3XL
Thread: Black 6/0
Tail and Antennae: White rubber
Rib: Yellow monocord
Abdomen: Yellow chenille
Back and Thorax: Black chenille
Hackle: Gray ostrich under brown

Whether used as an attractor or as a stonefly nymph, this fly should be in every fly box in good supply for fishing Montana streams. The rubber tail and antennae add terrific action to this fly, often triggering strikes. Weight heavily for fast-moving or deep rivers. Brown-over-orange bodies are also very effective.

Stoneflies

Brooks' Montana Stone
Hook: #4-12, Wet Fly, 2-4XL
Thread: Black 6/0
Tail: Black biots
Rib: Brown V-Rib
Body: Black fuzzy yarn
Hackle: Grizzly and brown
Gills: Ostrich herl

Originator: Charles Brooks, West Yellowstone, Mont.

This big, easy-to-tie pattern was created in 1958 to suggest salmonfly nymphs. Although there are more exact imitations, this pattern and its "in-the-round" silhouette are highly effective at fooling large trout. Small versions of this pattern make excellent imitations of tiny winter stonefly nymphs. Stonefly nymph patterns are usually weighted and fished close to the bottom.

Girdle Bug
Hook: #2-10, Wet Fly, 3-6XL
Thread: Black 3/0
Tail and Legs: White rubber
Body: Black chenille

This highly popular pattern mimics stoneflies and other aquatic organisms of Northwest rivers and streams. The action of this fly serves as an attractor for large fish. It is tied heavily weighted with brown, yellow, or orange chenille used as substitute colors or woven in as a contrasting underbody. Various sizes produce durable imitations of many stonefly groups. A popular variation adds a grizzly hackle palmered over the body and reinforced with a wire rib.

Golden Stonefly Nymph
Hook: #6-8, Wet Fly, 2-3XL
Thread: Yellow gold 3/0
Tail: Goose biots
Body: Yellow gold dubbing
Rib: Gold Swannundaze
Wingcase: Turkey tail
Legs: Yellow gold hackle

Originator: Joe King, Spokane, Wash.

Golden stonefly nymphs emerge in Northwest waters from mid-May through June, depending on the water temperature. Local hatches of golden stoneflies often last only a week, usually beginning near the river mouth and progressing upstream to the headwaters. A larger version of this pattern tied in black imitates the giant black stonefly nymphs. Both should be heavily weighted and fished dead-drift near the bottom.

Kaufmann's Black Stone

Hook: #2-10, Wet Fly, 2-6XL
Thread: Black 3/0
Tail: Brown goose biots
Rib: Black Swannundaze
Body: Mixed Angora goat
Wingcase: Black turkey quill
Antennae: Brown goose biots

Originator: Randall Kaufmann, Portland, Ore.

This is one of the best stonefly patterns for Western rivers. The pattern is both durable and realistic with a sleek, striking silhouette. It was originally tied with seal fur, but mixed brown, claret, and black Angora goat is an effective substitute. This pattern is also effective for steelhead. It is usually fished weighted close to the bottom, "dead-drift style." When the strike indicator hesitates, it's time to set the hook.

Little Yellow Stone

Hooks: #10-14, Wet Fly, 2-4XL
Thread: Light yellow 3/0
Wingcase: Dyed pheasant flank
Rib: Light yellow thread
Body: Chartreuse wool yarn
Tail and Hackle: Dyed mallard

Originator: Polly Rosborough, Chiloquin, Ore.

This pattern is used to simulate little yellow and green stonefly nymphs. It is tied with yellow to chartreuse to pale olive-green yarn and hackle. It is usually weighted with six to eight turns of fine non-lead wire over the hook and is fished through the summer. It can also be fished as an unweighted dropper fly beneath dry-fly patterns to lure selective trout when fishing pressure is heavy.

Montana Nymph

Hook: #6-10, Wet Fly, 2-3XL
Thread: Black 3/0
Tail: Black hackle fibers
Rib: Gold wire
Body: Black chenille
Legs: Black saddle hackle
Thorax: Black and yellow chenille

This stonefly pattern is particularly popular in the fast-flowing streams of the Northwest. This durable pattern should be heavily weighted and tied as single color or in mixed combinations of black, brown, yellow, or orange. The two strands of black chenille over the thorax are pulled forward after palmering the hackle.

Prince Nymph
Hooks: #6-10, Wet Fly, 2-3XL
Thread: Black 6/0
Tail: Brown goose biots
Rib: Gold tinsel, fine
Body: Peacock herl
Wing: White goose biots
Hackle: Brown, soft

Originator: Doug Prince, Visalia, Calif.

The Prince Nymph, originated in 1941, has certainly stood the test of time. It is a simple but effective pattern which presents a basic stonefly nymph silhouette. Variations in size and color produce imitations of many small to mid-sized stonefly nymphs. The recent addition of a bead head to this pattern has proved highly effective.

T-bur Stone
Hook: #10-14, Wet Fly, 2XL
Thread: Red or orange 6/0
Tail: Brown or red goose biots
Rib: Copper wire, medium
Body: Antron dubbing
Lateral Wing: Pearl tinsel

Originator: Tim Tollett, Dillon, Mont.

This fly represents the little yellow or olive stoneflies, but is also effective during caddis and mayfly hatches. It can be fished weighted or unweighted. The lateral flash wingcase is tied on using a single strand of #10 or 12 flat pearl tinsel trimmed as shown. Bead-head versions are also used. Color variations include yellow-green, olive, and brown-black.

Stonefly Adults

Improved Sofa Pillow
Hooks: #4-10, Dry Fly, 2-3XL
Thread: Orange 3/0
Tail: Elk hair
Rib: Orange thread
Body: Burnt orange poly yarn
Wing: Elk hair
Hackle: Brown

Originators: Pat and Sig Barnes, West Yellowstone, Mont.

This improved version of the Sofa Pillow is an easily tied, high-floating imitation for salmonflies hatching on large Western rivers. Size and color variations produce suitable imitations for various large to mid-sized stonefly adults. Variations include an orange tail with a scarlet yarn body, and combinations of olive-green to brown-black bodies.

MacSalmon

Hooks: #6-8, Dry Fly, 2-3XL
Thread: Orange 3/0
Body: Orange macramé cord
Underwing: Turkey fly sheet
Overwing: Cream elk hair
Collar and Head: Brown deer hair

Originator: Al Troth, Dillon, Mont.
The MacSalmon fly is a very durable and buoyant pattern. Variation in the color and size provides effective imitations for many of the larger stonefly species. A yellow body and wing version with the addition of rubber legs produces an effective grasshopper imitation, the MacHopper.

Riverbend Olive Stone

Hooks: #6-10, Dry Fly, 2-3XL
Thread: Olive monocord 3/0
Tail: Olive-dyed elk hair
Body: Brown-olive dubbing
Underwing: Brown-dyed elk
Overwing: White calf
Hackle: Olive grizzly saddle

Originator: Chuck Stranahan, Hamilton, Mont.
This pattern was originally tied to imitate the pre-runoff stoneflies that hatch on the Bitterroot and Clark Fork rivers of Montana in April.

Variations in color and size of this recipe produce effective patterns for many small to mid-size stoneflies through the spring and summer. The low-rider silhouette is produced by clipping the hackle on its undersurface. Butt sections from tail and wing are tied down as underbody for increased buoyancy.

Yellow Sally

Hook: #14-16, Dry Fly
Thread: Yellow 6/0-8/0
Body: Yellow round foam
Wing: Yellow Fly Sheet
Hackle: Yellow saddle

Originator: G.L. Britton, Spokane, Wash.
This is an excellent dry-fly imitation for yellow to olive-green stoneflies on Western rivers and streams. These flies emerge in the late afternoon and into the evening on warm days. The closed-cell foam body provides a durable fly that doesn't need contin-

ual dressing during the fast period of a hatch. Clip hackle on underside to make fly rest flat on the water's surface. Yellow or green dubbing is added under hackle for coloration.

Terrestrials:
The Land-dwelling Insects

*A*fter the major aquatic hatches of spring and early summer have subsided, fish are forced to become more opportunistic and to feed on insects that fall into their realm. A large number of these insects are terrestrials.

Terrestrials greatly outnumber the aquatic insects more commonly associated with fly-fishing, such as the mayflies, stoneflies, and caddisflies, but because they're primarily land dwellers, they're available to fish only intermittently, usually during mid- to late summer, when they're most abundant and active.

Ants, Beetles, and Grasshoppers

Lush vegetation along waterways contains large numbers of crawling and flying insects. Like a magnet, the water draws life to its edges and traps many unfortunate bees, beetles, grasshoppers, and ants when they fall onto its surface. High winds and rainstorms can drive hundreds of terrestrials to the water and attract both trout and trout fishers alike. Some anglers repeatedly cast terrestrial imitations into unproductive water in hopes of initiating their own feeding frenzy. Others have been known to shake bushes and trees along their favorite streams to stimulate the appetite of trout.

Unlike adult aquatic insects, terrestrials have relatively large bodies and feet adapted for dry-land locomotion, rather than for skimming across the water. Unfortunate terrestrials that fall into lakes and streams are trapped by the surface tension of the water. The insects initially float because their bodies are lighter than water. They frequently struggle to free themselves, attracting fish.

Submerged Insects

Terrestrials floating on the surface present a highly visible, full-body silhouette to fish. Eventually, the respiratory systems of the insects become saturated with water and they begin to sink. Often, especially in streams that are heavily fished, terrestrial patterns are taken more readily once they have become submerged. Some anglers simultaneously fish both a wet and a dry version of their favorite terrestrial, by using a dropper. (See Britton I and II for dropper setup.)

Unlike flying adult aquatic insects at the end of their life cycle, terrestrials eaten by trout are usually actively feeding insects in the prime of their life and have very high nutritional value. Trout seem to appreciate this and will go out of their way to snatch a beetle floating by during the middle of a stonefly hatch.

Fishing Techniques

Terrestrial imitations are usually fished on, or just below, the surface of the water with dry or intermediate lines. On stillwaters, imitations should occasionally be twitched to enhance their attraction. In moving water, dry patterns should be cast upstream and allowed to float back toward the angler in a realistic, "dead-drift" style. A realistic presentation is achieved when the fly follows the same course and speed of a natural insect caught in the current. This requires the fly fisher to retrieve the fly line as it floats downstream. Anglers must not allow drag from the line to cause any deviation in the fly's natural path as it floats in the current.

Variations

The terrestrial group of insects includes numerous families of bugs that have distinct shapes and color patterns. Variations in the size and color of specific families of terrestrials are often seen in different regions and at different times of the year. Fly fishers must consult local experts or undertake on-site field examinations of local insect populations to determine which terrestrial patterns will work best.

This chapter offers some of the more common terrestrial patterns found in the Northwest. It is by no means a complete listing of the insect types occurring in this region. The patterns in this book should be used as a starting point. Fly tiers should evaluate each pattern and modify its characteristics to suit their specific needs.

Gerald Almy's book, *Tying and Fishing Terrestrials*, offers plenty of additional information on terrestrials.

Deer Hair Beetle

Hook: #8-18, Dry Fly
Thread: Black 6/0
Legs *and Wingcase:* Black deer
Underbody: Black dubbing

This is a standard fly pattern for your box. It is very effective in both still- and moving-water conditions. It makes a realistic imitation of Crowe beetles when tied in smaller sizes, and stinkbugs when tied in larger sizes. The pattern is especially effective in the fall around wooded lakes. Brightly colored Antron may be added for increased visibility.

Flying Fur Ant

Hook: #8-10, Dry Fly
Thread: Brown 6/0
Body: Brown fur dubbed
Hackle: Furnace
Wing: Ginger hackle tips

Wings have been added to this pattern to match the flying ant which migrates in the Inland Northwest from mid-April through May. Non-winged versions fished dry or just beneath the surface work well throughout the summer in lakes and streams. Black or brown abdomens with orange-brown thorax versions are also popular.

Foam Ant

Hook: #14-16, Dry Fly
Thread: Black 6/0
Body: Black round foam
Hackle: Black neck or saddle

Ants are found throughout the Northwest and are readily eaten by opportunistic trout. This foam pattern is easily tied, floats well, and with the white tip is highly visible. Fish it all summer when exploring new water or when nothing appears to be hatching. Make a thread base on the hook for securing the foam body and a wider than normal thread foundation for the hackle.

Foam Beetle

Hook: # 6-18, Dry Fly
Thread: Black 6/0
Overbody: Black foam
Body: Peacock herl
Legs: Black deer hair

This is a simple, durable beetle imitation that won't sink. An indicator of brightly colored poly yarn or foam is added as shown to increase visibility. This is another searching pattern which is effective all summer. Be sure to use only closed-cell foam for dry-fly patterns.

Terrestrials

Improved Roope's Hopper

Hook: #8-10, Dry Fly, 2-3XL
Thread: Brown 6/0
Body: Yellow closed-cell foam
Underwing: Deer hair, fine
Wing: Turkey tail
Head: Deer hair
Legs: Yellow round rubber

Originator: Joe Roope, Coeur d'Alene, Ida.

An excellent hopper for Idaho and Montana streams in July and August. Cast into riffles, and when the hopper floats into slack-water, twitch the rod tip to impart action to the legs. Streams with grassy banks are best bets. Bright-colored foam may be added as an overwing to increase visibility. The turkey tail wing is covered with thinned Shoe-Goo for durability. Wet-fly hooks can also be used.

Jay–Dave's Hopper

Hook: #4-14, Dry Fly, 2-3XL
Thread: Yellow 6/0
Tail: Red deer hair
Body: Yellow poly yarn
Rib: Brown hackle
Underwing: Yellow deer hair
Overwing: Turkey wing quill
Legs: Yellow grizzly
Collar and Head: Deer hair

Originator: Dave Whitlock, Mountain Home, Ark.

Whitlock designed this hopper, without legs, in 1972. Later Jay Buchner added legs of knotted pheasant tail fibers. Now, many tiers make more easily knotted legs with trimmed, yellow-dyed, grizzly saddle hackle. A short loop of yarn extends past the hook bend and is part of the tail. Closed-cell foam may also be used as body. All-black versions are also effective.

Parachute Hopper

Hook: #6-12, Dry Fly, 2XL
Thread: Brown 6/0
Tail: Deer hair, fine
Body: Green dubbed
Post: White poly
Wing: Turkey wing
Legs: Pheasant tail fibers
Thorax: Olive dubbing
Hackle: Grizzly

Grasshoppers are abundant in the Northwest from July through September. Large trout feed on these insects from mid-morning until dark. This parachute-style pattern sits low in the water and is very effective in slow, smooth-water areas of rivers and streams. Cast the fly hard to the surface to create a disturbance and occasionally give the rod tip a twitch to wiggle the floating fly. With this pattern, hot windy days are best.

Crustaceans:
Hard-shelled Invertebrates

*T*his chapter covers imitations of scuds, crayfish and snails. All are common in Northwest lakes and slow-water areas of rivers and streams. They are usually found in water less than 15 feet deep. These creatures are most active during the night and in low-light early and late in the day. Crustaceans are most available throughout the spring, summer, and fall seasons.

Freshwater Shrimp: Scuds

Scuds are freshwater shrimp found in many lakes, usually in good abundance. Imitations should be fished with a slow hand-twist retrieve, occasionally adding a quick 6- to 12-inch strip or two. Depending on water depth, floating, intermediate or sinking lines are used to hold the fly close to the bottom. Colors include various shades of yellow-tan to green, gray and brown, and can differ from lake to lake. Sizes range from 1/4 to one inch.

Crayfish

Crayfish patterns are fished on or near the bottom, close to weed beds and rocky shorelines. Realistic patterns tied on keel hooks with dumbbell eyes ride with the hook point up where it won't snag. This allows the pattern to be retrieved slowly along the bottom. Impressionistic patterns, such as the Crayfish Leech or orange-brown Woolly Buggers, imitate backward-swimming crayfish and are fished with quick, 10- to 20-inch strips close to the bottom. Fish prefer to attack small, young, swimming crayfish whose pinchers are small and ineffective. Colors include rusty orange to olive-brown with lighter coloration on the under surface.

Snails

Snails are present in many lakes and slow-moving streams. Weighted patterns are cast out over weed beds and allowed to sink close to the bottom. They are retrieved with a slow hand twist. Intermittently the rod tip is raised two to three feet, then dropped back to the surface of the water, allowing the pattern to fall back close to the bottom. Fish pick up the fly softly, often as it sinks downward. The pattern shown also works well under strike indicators, especially when there is wave action on the water's surface.

Aquatic Insects and Their Imitations, For All North America by Rick Hafele and Scott Roederer provides additional information on crustaceans.

Crustaceans, Snail

Peacock Snail
Hook: #10-14, Wet Fly
Thread: Brown or black, 6/0
Hackle: Stiff brown saddle
Rib: Copper wire
Body: Peacock herl

Originator: Gary Borger, Wausau, Wis.
This improved pattern is usually fished heavily weighted, but an unweighted version may be used on warm days when snails can be seen floating on the surface. The copper wire is twisted in with the peacock herl to protect the herl and form a robust body.

Crustaceans, Crayfish

Brown Lead Head
Hook: #4-6, Wet Fly, 2-4XL
Thread: Brown 3/0
Tail: Chickabou feathers
Rib: Copper wire, fine
Hackle: Saddle, palmered
Eyes: Dumbbell
Body: Crystal Chenille

Popular all over western Montana, this fly's heavy eyes sink the pattern quickly with the hook point up. Cast with caution using the "chuck and duck" technique. Fish the fly dead-drift, bouncing it along the bottom, or with a quick, crayfish-style retrieve. Colors include green, gray, olive, orange, brown, and purple.

Chickabou Crayfish
Hook: #4-10, Wet Fly, 4-6XL
Thread: Brown 3/0
Eyes: Monofilament at bend
Tail: Brown flank feather
Body: Brown Chickabou, clipped
Legs: Brown Chickabou, palmered

Originator: Henry Hoffman,
Warrenton, Ore.
A soft-body crayfish pattern made with dyed grizzly underbelly feathers marketed under the trade name Chickabou and others. This pattern can be used in lakes and streams. It should be fished on the bottom. A hook-point-up retrieve is accomplished by positioning a painted dumbbell and wire weight on top of the hook.

Crustaceans

Crayfish Leech

Hook: #6-8, Wet Fly, 2-3XL
Thread: Brown 6/0
Body: Crayfish orange rabbit
Wing: Copper Krystal Flash
Hackle: Pheasant rump

This fly is an impressionistic pattern of a fleeing crayfish. It's tied weighted and is fished in shallow, weedbed areas with quick-strip retrieves of 6 to 18 inches. It's effective in most shallow lowland lakes. Heavily weighted patterns are effective in slow-moving sections of rivers and streams. Color combinations vary from rusty brown to dark green-brown depending on the color of the lake bottom. Use cross-cut rabbit strips to wrap the body.

Immature Crayfish

Hook: #10-12, Wet Fly, 2-3XL
Thread: Black 3/0
Tail: Black marabou
Overshell: Pearl Flashabou
Rib: Gold wire, fine
Body: Green-black fur, dubbed
Legs: Black pheasant rump

Originator: Ben Wolen, Cheney, Wash.
This fly pattern is intended to represent small juvenile crayfish in basalt-bottomed eastern Washington lakes and streams. The fly may be tied weighted and should be fished right on the bottom with a quick hand-twist retrieve. The dubbed fur is 80 percent rabbit and 20 percent African goat. Red-orange fur and brown pheasant rump feathers also work well.

Crustaceans, Scuds

Clipped Scud

Hook: #8-16, Scud
Thread: Yellow 6/0
Body: Hare's ear dubbing

Popularized: Tom Wendelberg
Pick out guard hairs for antennae, legs, and tail. Clip top and sides as shown. Can be tied partway down curve of hook or only on straight section of shank. Colors include pale shades of tan, olive green, pink, and orange mixed to match naturals. This pattern is very effective in lakes and slow-moving streams with slow hand-twist retrieves and occasional quick strips.

Nyerges Nymph
Hook: #8-10, Wet Fly, 2-3XL
Thread: Black 6/0
Hackle: Brown, palmered
Body: Dark olive chenille

Originator: Gil Nyerges, Bothell, Wash.

This is a simple, durable, and extremely effective pattern for Columbia Basin lakes, and it is highly popular in northeast Washington. It suggests olive shrimps and nymphs. It is most effective when large scuds are active along shorelines. Retrieve with a steady hand-twist and intermittent short quick strips. Clip top and sides of palmered hackle to form shrimp appearance.

Pittman's Scud
Hook: #6-18, Wet Fly, 2XL
Thread: Olive 6/0 Monocord
Tail: Olive mallard flank
Rib: Monofilament
Shell: Plastic bag strip
Body: Olive rabbit and Antron

Originator: Joe Pittman, Burien, Wash.

Swimming scuds have a straight body appearance as suggested by this perennial favorite fly. Freshwater shrimp use their legs to swim forward and whip their tails to dart backward. Retrieve this fly with your rod at an angle to the fly line because scud-feeding fish strike hard. Other colors include gray, light brown, pink, and orange. Pick hairs from underbody to form legs.

Aquatic Bugs

When most major aquatic hatches are over in the fall, backswimmers and water boatmen are just reaching maturity and will winter in the water as adults. Although the adults can fly, they continue to live under water until spring, providing a good source of food for trout during the lean fall and winter months. As a result, these insects are attracting the attention of an increasing number of fly fishers.

Because they are similar in appearance, habits, and habitat, the water boatmen patterns presented here also represent backswimmers.

Naturals

These aquatic bugs breathe atmospheric oxygen and carry a bubble of air with them when they dive under the water. They thrive along vegetated shorelines in shallow, weedy areas in most lakes and ponds and in the slack marginal water of streams.

Water boatmen average 1/4 to 1/2 inch in length, whereas backswimmers are slightly larger and more elongated. Their appearance has been likened to a flattened football or, in the case of water boatmen, a small boat complete with oars. Of course, backswimmers swim on their backs. Water boatmen are often called simply "boatmen" by fly fishers.

Body colors match the insects' surroundings. Shades of green, brown and tan are common. The belly is lighter than the rest of the body. Three sets of legs serve different functions. The bugs use their short front legs to collect food, the middle legs to grasp, and use their hind, long, paddle-shaped legs, which have a fringe of swimming hair, to propel themselves in short one-third-inch, jerky, sculling movements.

Often as early as February, adults take flight to mate and to colonize new water. They

return to the water to lay eggs, then later die. The eggs hatch and the nymphs grow during the spring and summer months when fish are more interested in other food sources.

Imitations and Presentation

The air these insects collect for underwater use is trapped under their wings and along the underside of their abdomens, making their bodies glisten like silver as they dart through the water. A trail of small bubbles might follow them. Patterns should emphasize this visible characteristic by incorporating sparkle yarn, tinsel, or other shiny materials.

In *Designing Trout Flies*, Gary Borger states that he prefers a standard soft-hackle fly such as a #12-16 Sparkle Caddis Pupa dressed in smoky gray. He believes the trout don't see a motionless bug with outstretched legs. They see a sculling, glowing caricature, not detail.

Retrieve with short, fast strips to mimic the natural's jerky up-and-down movements. At rest, backswimmers hang their heads down just under the surface with their oar-like legs outstretched in wait of prey. In this position they become easy prey for cruising fish. An unweighted imitation fished on a floating line and greased leader is highly effective when trout are plucking backswimmers from the surface film.

Additional information on these interesting insects is found in *The Complete Book of Western Hatches* by Rick Hafele and Dave Hughes and *Aquatic Entomology* by W. Patrick McCafferty.

Bead Head Flashback Water Boatman

Hook: #12, Dry Fly
Head: Gold Brite Bead, 1/8"
Thread: Black 8/0
Rib: Silver wire
Shellback: Pearl Flashabou
Body: Peacock herl
Legs: Black or white round rubber
Collar: Peacock herl

Originator: Jan Sadlo, Spokane, Wash.
The bead head gives the sparkle created in the natural by trapped air and also provides weight that helps give the up-down darting action of the natural when the fly is retrieved. The 1/4-inch-wide pearlescent ribbon shellback simulates trapped air beneath the natural's wings.

Bubbler Boatman

Hook: #12, Wet Fly
Thread: Black 6/0
Tail: Krystal Flash
Shellback: Olive turkey tail
Body: Peacock green chenille
Legs: Black round rubber

Originator: Frank E. Knapp Jr., Colbert, Wash.
Attach a strip of non-lead wire on each side of the hook shank for weight and to create a wide body. Two strands of Krystal Flash at the tail simulates streams of bubbles, which trail behind a diving boatman. This pattern has proven very effective when cast near shorelines during the fall or early spring.

Water Boatman

Hook: #10-12, Dry Fly
Thread: Black 3/0
Underbody: Black wool
Eyes: Black medium mono
Overbody and Highlight: See below
Body: Peacock herl
Legs: Black goose biots
Head: Peacock herl

Originator: John Newbury, Chewelah, Wash.
This beautiful and realistic pattern has proven highly effective. It is worth the extra time required to tie it. Attach overbody of bronze herls from peacock eye feather and wind thread over them to the bend. Tie in pearlescent ribbon as underbody on bottom of hook. Add body herls and wrap forward. Secure pearlescent ribbon forward, attach legs, and then secure overbody behind eyes. Secure overbody herl again in front of eyes.

Aquatic Worms

U ntil recently fly fishers have not considered using worm imitations due to the stigma associated with the use of earthworms as bait. However, fly fishers now know that aquatic worms live in sand and silt on the bottom of streams, and success stories with the fly pattern called the San Juan Worm have some fly-fishing purists accepting worm imitations. Add the word "aquatic" to a lowly worm and suddenly it becomes a respectable fly pattern.

Naturals

Aquatic worms are similar in appearance to earthworms or manure worms, but are only 3/4 to 1 1/2 inches in length and brighter in color. The natural color of aquatic worms is rusty brown, but at certain times they turn yellow. In addition to living on stream bottoms, they are abundant in spring creeks and tail waters.

Smaller red worms, known as bloodworms, are found primarily in stillwater and are actually the larval form of blood red Chironomids. Fish take both aquatic worms and Chironomid larvae readily. The imitations featured in this section and the Chironomid section are highly successful.

Patterns and Presentation

Patterns tied with a variety of materials such as marabou, Larva Lace, yarn, floss and Ultra Chenille are effective. Dyed leather or chamois becomes softer than Ultra Chenille when wet and makes very effective imitations. Most patterns call for the humped-back English bait hook to give the fly a natural curved appearance and to impart a seductive twisting as the fly sinks or drifts. Large sizes of this hook aren't recommended due to their tendency to pierce a fish's brain or eye. Bright red is a popular color because it doubles for annelids and the red midge larvae. Fluorescent orange and pink patterns ribbed with silver wire are also effective.

Aquatic worm patterns are effective in both rivers and in slow-moving spring creeks. Also, they're good for lake fishing. They don't swim, but when dislodged, they drift and tumble along the bottom with the current. Imitations should be presented in the same manner. A supple leader attached to the fly with a Duncan loop or uni-knot permits greater movement of the fly. A strike indicator keeps the worm at the right depth in addition to helping the fisherman detect strikes.

Designing Trout Flies by Gary Borger is a good source of additional information on aquatic worms.

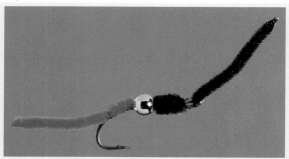

Bead Body Worm
Hook: #12, Dry Fly, 2XL
Bead: Copper, medium
Thread: Red 6/0
Front Body: Brown chenille
Wire: Red copper, medium
Rear Body: Red chenille

Originator: Don Richards, Livingston, Mont.
The use of a bead to simulate the annulus ring characteristic of worms seems to be a natural. Although a two-tone worm might not seem logical, it has been a fantastic producer and has taken many trophy trout. Fine, 1/16-inch chenille is used for the body, and the bead may be gold or silver. A scud hook may also be used.

Bionic Worm
Hooks: #10-14, Scud
Thread: Red 6/0
Tail: Red marabou
Body: Bright red

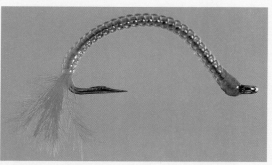

The Bionic Worm was designed to mimic the bloodworm, a Chironomid larva, but it might also be taken as an annelid or a small leech. It has become very popular with Inland Northwest fly fishers on stillwaters, where fish gorge themselves on bloodworms in the spring and fall. As this pattern will sink quickly, there is no need to weight it. The body may be of V-Rib, Swannundaze or Body Glass.

San Juan Worm
Hooks: #6-10, Scud
Thread: Red flat waxed nylon
Underbody: Red thread
Overbody: Red Ultra-Chenille

This pattern was first popularized on the San Juan River's fabulous tailwater fishery below the Navajo Dam in northern New Mexico, but it has since proven highly effective on both streams and stillwaters across the Northwest. Other popular colors include tan, orange, purple, and brown. A yarn-body variant ribbed with silver or copper wire can be used as a scud pattern.

Leeches

L eeches are one of the most important—but least understood—items on a trout's menu. So far, more than 650 species of leeches are known; about 45 freshwater species exist in the United States.

Naturals

Leeches can walk like inchworms, using strong fore and aft suckers, or stretch themselves into ribbons and swim with a smooth and rhythmic up-and-down undulation at a speed of about one foot per two or three seconds. When fully extended, they can attain lengths of six inches or more. Northwest leeches are predominately dark brown, black, olive or mottled green and black. Some are spotted, mottled, streaked or striped in reds, oranges, or yellow.

Leeches prefer the shallow water of streams, lakes and ponds, usually less than six feet deep. They hide under vegetation, rocks or debris and feed on dead or decaying organic matter. They are usually nocturnal, but venture out in the morning and evening. Occasionally, they're seen swimming just beneath the surface of the water in broad daylight.

Imitations

A wide variety of patterns has been developed to imitate the leech. An early pattern consisted of a black wool body with a long, black, bear-hair tail; it caught trout. Since undulation is an important characteristic, many effective patterns use marabou or other soft, flexible materials. It is also thought that some feather-wing streamers are taken for leeches.

A strip of fur cut from a tanned hide tied in Matuka-style or wrapped around the hook and extending behind the hook, as in the Bunny Leech, can be used to impart the fluid

Leeches

up-and-down movement of a swimming leech. A strip of chamois dyed to match naturals is effective also. Wrapped Mohair-yarn patterns with the fibers brushed back are simple to tie yet very effective.

The mottled appearance of leeches has prompted many tiers to use variegated chenilles and spectrumized colors of Mohair. Woolly Buggers, such as the Halloween Leech, which are heavily weighted in the front, sink headfirst during pauses in the retrieve causing the marabou tail to undulate. Most patterns call for a tail that is 1 or 1 1/2 times the length of the hook. Imitations don't have to be as long as mature adult leeches because fish prefer to eat younger leeches that are one to two inches long. Tie leeches in various sizes. Sometimes trout will refuse large offerings but take smaller sizes, such as a #12, 2XL.

Presentation

Leech patterns are usually fished slow and deep with a jigging retrieve or a slow, steady hand twist. An active retrieve with twitching, pumping and varying speeds may be the ticket in stillwater. In streams, cast the fly across and upstream, then mend the line to keep it drifting sideways to the current or bounce it off the bottom, dead-drift.

If you get short hits, continue retrieving until the fish comes back for a solid take or try shortening the tail a little. Keep experimenting to find the best action for given circumstances.

Leeches are prevalent year-round, but are more active in the spring and fall. Fish will take a leech any time of day although evenings and early mornings are most productive. Another good time to fish leeches is at night during the summer.

Additional information on leeches can be found in *Naturals, A Guide to Food Organisms of the Trout*, 1980, and *Designing Trout Flies*, 1991, by Gary Borger.

Bunny Leech
Hooks: #4-8, Wet Fly, 2-3XL
Thread: Black 3/0
Weight: Front half only
Tail and Body: Rabbit hide

A thin strip of black, purple or olive cross-cut tanned rabbit hide with hair left on is tied tightly at back of hook, with a tail equal to the hook length. Wrap remainder forward in connecting spirals, pulling fur back with each wrap. Secure at eye. Dumbbell eyes can be added as weight. Vary the retrieve to learn what works in both fast and stillwater settings.

Cactus Chenille Leech

Hooks: #4-8, Wet Fly, 2-4XL
Thread: Black 3/0
Weight: Front third
Tail: Black marabou
Body: Black Cactus Chenille

Originator: Ron Brown, Livingston, Mont.

Weighting and bending the front one-third of the hook down slightly gives an undulating motion when the fly is stripped slowly. The Cactus Chenille is wound tightly and trimmed on top and bottom to provide a flat silhouette. It is also trimmed in a tapered and diamond shape for leech-like silhouette. This fly has produced good results in lakes across the country. Commercially bent shank hooks are available.

Halloween Leech

Hooks: #4-8, Wet Fly, 2-3XL
Head: Black bead
Thread: Black 3/0
Tail: Black marabou
Rib: Copper wire
Hackle: Black saddle, palmered
Body: Variegated chenille

Originator: Bill Schiess, Henry's Lake, Ida.

The popularity of this simple pattern is now spreading throughout the Northwest. Newer variations call for a rusty brown marabou tail, brown and orange variegated chenille body, and a brown or furnace palmered saddle hackle. Some tiers add strands of pearl or orange Krystal Flash to the tail. The brown Halloween is probably taken as a crayfish. The bead head is optional on this Woolly Bugger variation.

Mohair Leech

Hooks: #4-14, Wet Fly, 3-6XL
Thread: 3/0 color of body
Tail: Mohair fibers
Body: Mohair yarn

Black, medium to dark brown, olive, reddish brown, magenta and maroon yarns are most popular. Canadian Series Mohairs, spectrumized colors, are very effective. The maroon version shown was popularized by Jack Shaw, of Kamloops, B.C., and is known in Canada as the highly effective "Blood Leech." The secret to the "swept back" appearance of the fly is to stroke the Mohair up and back towards the tail continuously as the yarn is wrapped forward.

Streamers

A t certain times of the year in most waters, large numbers of small fish outgrow the protection of shoreline weed beds and venture into deeper waters. There, usually in schools, they become available to larger fish. The predators sometimes target inattentive or injured minnows within these schools as they require the least amount of energy to pursue. Minnows are also pursued out of curiosity or in an attempt by larger fish to dominate a particular area.

Early anglers discovered that large fish could be fooled into striking crude streamer patterns constructed with a few feathers tied to a bare hook. Over the years the concept of large fish being caught on streamer patterns hasn't changed, but the patterns have evolved into highly effective, often very realistic imitations and even elaborate works of art such as Atlantic salmon flies. As with aquatic insects, proper size, color, and an accurate silhouette make for the best streamer patterns.

The patterns selected for this chapter are good examples of the basic streamers needed to round out a fly box. Various materials and tying techniques are illustrated. Many of the patterns have been used for decades. Updated versions incorporating some of the flashy new tying materials are shown. Fly tiers are encouraged to experiment with new materials and color combinations when tying these basic patterns, keeping in mind the characteristics of the natural. Discovering an effective new variation of a basic pattern in itself is a thrill, and also helps to build an angler's confidence.

Using different streamer patterns, fly fishers learn to understand the function of various fly-tying components and their ability to attract fish. The same streamer pattern will not work as well in both still and moving water without some modification. For example, substitution of a soft marabou wing for a stiff bucktail wing can add lifelike movement to a fly fished in stillwaters. Conversely, more durable bucktail is often substituted for marabou on flies to be used in rough waters. The most effective color combination for a particular pattern often depends upon light conditions. In general, brightly colored flies work best on sunny days and darker flies work best during low light.

Minnow Characteristics

Presentation of streamer patterns is critical when using streamers. The angler needs to become well acquainted with the life cycle and habitat of the minnow. Additional attention should be paid to their day-to-day movements and style of swimming. Are they bottom-feeding sculpins or tightly schooled threadfin shad? Depending on the depth at which minnows are found, fly fishers use various casting techniques as well as a full complement of dry and sinking lines and weighted and unweighted flies to achieve a natural presentation.

Retrieves

In clear lakes and streams, anglers wearing polarized glasses can see the action that various retrieves give to a fly. Slow, steady strips and fast, erratic retrieves mimic various swimming and darting motions. Abrupt changes in the direction and speed of a retrieve, or simply leaving the fly motionless for several seconds, can trigger fish to strike.

In fast-moving water, minnows swept downstream in the current swim to the safety of the shoreline as soon as possible. This natural tendency can be imitated by casting streamer patterns out into the current at a 45 degree angle from straight downstream and allowing the fly to swing back toward the shore. In heavy current an upstream mend in the fly line keeps the fly moving through the swing at an even speed.

Strikes usually occur during the swing or as the fly is being retrieved. Most fish hook themselves on the moving fly and except for very large fish there is no need to set the hook. In slower-moving sections, streamers are often retrieved straight across the current or downstream with the current. Cross-current and upstream casts can also be used to fish weighted sculpin-type patterns close to the bottom. Anglers need only to step one or two paces downstream at the end of each cast or two to cover an entire riffle.

In stillwaters, streamers are most effective when fished with sink-tip or full-sinking lines along weed beds, drop-offs and at the mouths of inflowing streams. In most lakes, fish rest in cooler, deeper water and only move closer to the surface or shallow areas at feeding time. Early morning or late evening are often the best times to find larger fish feeding in such water.

Additional information can be found in *Streamers and Bucktails: The Big Fish Flies* by Joseph Bates.

Streamers

Black Nose Dace

Hook: #2-10, Wet Fly,
  2-4XL
Thread: Black 6/0
Tail: Red yarn
Rib: Silver oval tinsel
Body: Silver tinsel, wide
Wing: Bucktail

Originator: Art Flick,
Westkill, N.Y.
This time-tested basic streamer pattern was developed in the eastern U.S., but is known to be a very effective minnow imitation throughout the West.

The wing is tied thicker for use on larger flies and in heavy water. Weight is added to the front of the hook as needed. The wing combines brown over black over white bucktail.

Bucktail Coachman

Hook: #2-10, Wet Fly, 2-4XL
Thread: Black prewaxed
  6/0
Tail: Golden pheasant tippets
Body: Red floss, peacock
  herl
Wing: White bucktail
Hackle: Brown saddle, soft

This classic wet-fly is an adaptation of a historic English dressing used for generations. Both the dry and wet versions are excellent for trout and most other game fish.

Kiwi Muddler

Hook: #2-10, Wet Fly, 2-6XL
Thread: Tan prewaxed
  4/0
Tail: Natural deer hair
Rib: Silver oval tinsel
Body: Light tan wool
Wing: Natural rabbit
  strip
Collar and Head: Deer
  hair

This New Zealand-style fly is made with fur strips tied along the top of the fly body. The soft fur provides a realistic pulsating silhouette and is quite durable. It is tied in a variety of colors, including brown, black, green, yellow, and white. Add wire weight as desired.

Matuka Muddler

Hook: #2-10, Wet Fly, 2-6XL
Thread: Tan 6/0
Rib: Copper wire, fine
Body: Light tan foam
Wing: Brown grizzly hackles
Hackle: Brown grizzly hackle
Collar and Head: Dark deer hair
Eyes: Plastic beads

This style of streamer also comes from New Zealand, and was originally tied with matuka feathers. Dyed grizzly feathers have been substituted and are tied along the top of the hook, Matuka style. The body is colored with permanent markers to match native sculpins. The fly is heavily weighted and fished right on the bottom. Super Glue is squeezed into the deer hair head and allowed to dry. Plastic eyes are then glued onto the head.

Spruce

Hook: #2-10, Wet Fly, 2-4XL
Thread: Black monocord
Tail: Peacock sword
Body: Red wool and peacock herl
Wing: Badger, paired
Hackle: Badger

Originator: Bert Godfrey, Seaside, Ore.
An old-time Northwest streamer pattern used for trout, sea-run cutthroat, and steelhead. Also tied in a dark version using dark brown badger (furnace) hackle and wings.

Woolhead Sculpin

Hook: #2-10, Wet Fly, 2-6XL
Thread: Brown 6/0
Tail: Brown marabou
Body: Brown spun wool
Fins: Deer hair
Head: Brown spun wool

Originator: Ed Shenk, Carlisle, Penn.
This heavily weighted pattern is tied with materials that absorb water and make the fly sink rapidly.
Fish seem to hold onto this soft-bodied fly longer than they'll hold rigid sculpin patterns. This fly has a dark silhouette visible in low light and murky water. It should be fished slowly along the bottom of rivers and streams with good populations of sculpins.

Streamers

Yellow and White Streamer
Hook: #4-12, Wet Fly, 2-4XL
Thread: Yellow 6/0
Body: Gold Diamond Braid
Wing: Yellow and white bucktail

This streamer is a very simple pattern that takes spiny-ray fish when retrieved slowly and trout on a faster retrieve. The pattern shown is tied sparse for lake fishing; a thick wing version is used for moving water. Multiple color combinations of wing and body are used for this simple durable streamer pattern including silver, black, purple, red, and green.

Yellow Marabou Muddler
Hook: #2-8, Wet Fly, 2-6XL
Thread: Black 6/0
Tail: Red hackle fibers
Body: Silver Diamond Braid
Wing: Yellow marabou and peacock
Head: Deer hair

Originator: Dan Bailey, Livingston, Mont.
This version of the versatile Muddler has a large, clipped head that adds wiggle to the fly. Use of a loose-fitting knot like the Duncan loop keeps the

leader from impeding the fly's wiggle. The head also can be clipped flat on the sides or bottom to imitate thin minnows and sculpins. Variations include gold braid bodies and wing colors including white, black, brown, and green. Usually weighted.

Zonker
Hook: #2-6, Wet Fly, 2-6XL
Thread: White 6/0
Body: Pearl Mylar piping
Wing: Natural rabbit strip
Throat: Natural rabbit
Eyes: Painted black on yellow

This is a flashy variation of a fur-strip fly combining the soft pulsating action of white rabbit fur and the flash of pearl Mylar piping. It is an effective minnow imitation often tied with natural, pink, yellow, green, or black fur strips. The hook is usually weighted, and the Mylar piping should be glued over the hook as well as secured with tying thread.

Attractor, Multi-Purpose and Miscellaneous Patterns

Flies undoubtedly look a lot different from a fish's point of view. Many highly effective patterns don't look like anything natural from the human perspective, yet fish are attracted to them. Take the Royal Coachman, for example. When wet, the peacock body turns bronze and the band of red floss looks brown. What the fish sees is a brownish fly with a narrow waist that might look like an ant. Or maybe not. The point is, it works.

Some anglers feel that large and brightly colored attractor patterns stimulate a fish to strike out of curiosity, anger, or boredom. Others insist that fish don't have emotions, that they eat only to survive and take attractor flies out of reflex, that they will attack anything that resembles food. Bright colors do attract their attention and might evoke memories of something good to eat. When Lee Wulff was asked why fish take a Royal Wulff, he replied, "Well, I don't think they represent any one natural insect, but more a dessert, something after the main course, a little like strawberry shortcake. That's it, that's the best way I can describe my Royal Wulff, it looks like strawberry shortcake—something great big and juicy floating down to a large trout!"

Some flies are included in this section because they are difficult to classify, and others might imitate many food forms. Some are excellent "searching patterns" to use when there is no major hatch. These might serve as attractors, exciters, or noonday dredgers.

Dry-fly Attractors

Humpy
Hooks: #6-24, Dry Fly
Thread: Black 6/0 or 8/0
Tail: Moose or elk body hair
Overbody: Elk hair
Body: Floss or tying thread
Wing: Elk, tips of overbody
Hackle: Brown and grizzly

This elk-hair version is a great floating fly for the rougher waters of Western rivers and creeks. The Humpy and its cousin, the Goofus Bug, can also be tied with moose body hair. Floss or thread is wrapped over the butts of the elk-hair overbody before it is brought forward. Body colors are left to the tier: yellow, black, red, fluorescent green, chartreuse, or orange. The Royal Humpy has white calf-tail wings.

Renegade

Hooks: #8-16, Dry Fly
Thread: Black 6/0 or 8/0
Tag: Gold tinsel
Rear Hackle: Brown
Body: Peacock herl
Front Hackle: White

Originator: Taylor "Beartracks" Williams, Sun Valley, Ida.
The Renegade, which is nearly as popular as the Adams and the Royal Coachman, is a "must-have" pattern for anyone who fishes for cutthroat in the Northwest's lakes and streams. Other species of trout like it, too. It is highly visible, and because it is "symmetrical," it looks good from any angle. If fish don't take it dry, try fishing it subsurface.

Stimulator

Hooks: #4-18, Dry Fly, 2-3XL
Thread: Fire orange 6/0
Tail: Gray elk
Rib: Fine gold wire
Palmered Hackle: Brown
Body: Bright green Antron
Wing: Gray elk
Thorax: Amber goat
Front Hackle: Grizzly

Originator: Randall Kaufmann, Portland, Ore.
Stimulators can be tailored to match various caddis and stonefly hatches as well as hoppers. This pattern has gained enormous popularity because of its versatility. Alternate body colors are: black, golden, orange, yellow, and red.

The Bugmeister

Hooks: #8-12, Dry Fly, 2-3XL
Thread: Black 6/0
Tail: Elk hair
Post: White Z-lon
Body and Wing: Peacock herl
Wing: Elk hair and Krystal Flash
Hackle: Grizzly and brown

Originator: John Perry, Missoula, Mont.
This is an excellent searching pattern when there is no major hatch. Perry, who guides extensively on rivers in western Montana, uses it as a strike indicator when fishing nymphs or very small dry flies. It also is a good stonefly or hopper imitation. The wing includes elk hair over peacock herl and Krystal Flash.

Turck's Tarantula
Hooks: #4-12, Dry Fly, 2-3XL
Thread: Tan 3/0
Tail: Amherst pheasant tippet
Body: Dubbed hare's mask
Underwing: White calf tail
Overwing: Pearl Krystal Flash
Legs: White round rubber
Collar and Head: Deer body
    hair

Originator: Guy Turck,
Jackson Hole, Wyo.
Body color can be varied to
match hatches of big salmonflies, smaller stoneflies, grasshoppers, etc. Turck fishes the
Tarantula dead-drift but imparts some twitches as it enters the fish's window. This was the
fly pattern used by Joe Rupp to win the 1995 fishout at Jackson Hole, Wyoming.

Wright's Royal
Hooks: #10-16, Dry Fly
Thread: Black 6/0
Body: Peacock herl and red floss
Wing: Light elk hair
Hackle: Brown, palmered
Thorax: Peacock herl

Originator: Phil Wright, Livingston,
Mont.
This variation of the "Royal" family has
the profile of a terrestrial. The flared
elk-hair wing makes it an effective
caddis, hopper, or flying-ant imitation.
When 30 of the world's best fly tiers sub-
mitted their favorite patterns for *The
World's Best Trout Flies*, two chose
Wright's Royal.

Nymphs and Wet Flies

Don't Ask
Hooks: #8-10, Wet Fly, 2-3XL
Thread: Black 6/0
Tail: Pheasant tail fibers
Rib: Gold tinsel, fine
Body: Orange wool yarn
Hackle: Pheasant tail fibers

Originator: Alice Deaver,
Rathdrum, Ida.
Deaver thought she was tying
Carey Specials but mistakenly
used pheasant tail fibers instead
of a pheasant rump feather for the
hackle. The mistake proved to be a
highly effective fish taker. Pinches
of tail fibers are tied in on the top, bottom, and both sides. They may be adjusted to accommodate a variety of pattern sizes. Body color is tier's choice.

All Purpose Nymph
Hook: #12–16, Dry Fly
Thread: Brown 6/0
Tail: Olive Z-lon, crinkled
Rib: Copper wire, medium
Abdomen: Olive green dubbing
Wing: Bluish gray Z-lon
Antennae and Beard: Mallard
Head: Dark olive dubbing

Originator: John Perry, Missoula, Mont.
This fly is extremely versatile. It
can be fished anywhere from the bottom to the surface of moving waters, both dead-drift and on the swing. Try it as a dropper fly on a slow day. It imitates caddis, mayflies, and other food sources, including damselflies in lakes.

Dry Falls Gold
Hooks: #8-14, Wet Fly, 2XL
Thread: Dark brown 6/0
Tail: Golden pheasant tippet
Body: Gold-dyed yarn
Ribbing: Dark brown thread
Hackle: Brown–dyed grizzly

Originator: Jerry Harms, Spokane, Wash.
This fly, which produces fish from Opening Day to the last day of the season, is effective at many Inland Northwest lakes and streams. Harms retrieves it by using two quick, three- to six-inch strips, a three-second pause, followed by a single strip of three to six inches. Floating, sinking, or sink-tip lines all work well with this
pattern. Ribbing is a diamond pattern: wrap it from front to back and return.

Knudson's Gray Spider
Hooks: #10-12, Wet Fly, 2-3XL
Thread: Black 6/0
Tail: Mallard flank
Body: Yellow chenille
Hackle: Grizzly and mallard

Originator: Al Knudson, Everett, Wash.
Two to three stiff grizzly "under-hackles" prevent the mallard flank "over-hackle" from clinging to the body. The mallard flank feather is folded or turned over before being tied in and wound. The fly is best known as a sea-run cutthroat pattern, but is used for everything from steelhead in rivers to trout in inland lakes.

Runje's Leech
Hooks: #6-10, Wet Fly, 2-4XL
Thread: Brown 6/0
Tail: Red yarn
Body: Brown Mohair
Hackle: Pheasant rump

Originator: Mike Runje, Spokane, Wash.
After wrapping the Mohair body, pick out loose fibers to give the fly a buggy appearance. Inland Northwest fly fishers have caught a lot of fish on this easy-to-tie pattern. The fly is generally fished with a stripping retrieve on a fast-sinking line, but it works well at times when fished slowly using slow-sinking or even a floating line.

Sheep Creek Special
Hooks: #6-18, Wet Fly, 2-3XL
Thread: Black or olive 6/0
Hackle: Brown at rear
Body: Dark olive chenille
Wing: Mallard breast

Originator: George P. Biggs, Jerome, Ida.
Created in 1962, this is one of the basic flies in southern Idaho waters. Some consider it to be one of the best trout flies ever developed. Various shades of olive or brown chenille may be used for the body.

The Sword Tail
Hooks: #6-8, Wet Fly, 2-3XL
Thread: Black 6/0
Tail: Peacock sword fibers
Hackle: Blue dun saddle
Body: Black crystal chenille

Originator: Jerry Harms, Spokane, Wash.
This is an excellent grayling pattern. Rainbow and cutthroat love it, too. It has proved its effectiveness on Henry's Lake, Idaho, and many other lakes in the Northwest.

Woolly Worm
Hooks: #2-12, Wet Fly, 2-4XL
Thread: Black 6/0
Tail: Red yarn
Hackle: Grizzly saddle
Body: Dark olive chenille

Like the Woolly Bugger, the Woolly Worm is best considered a style of fly rather than a specific pattern. Variations in color and size suggest everything from leeches to scuds. Because it is symmetrical, it appears natural from any angle. Most anglers have a variety of these patterns in their boxes.

Zug Bug
Hooks: #6-16, Wet Fly, 2XL
Thread: Black 6/0
Tail: Peacock sword
Rib: Silver tinsel, oval
Body: Peacock herl
Hackle: Brown
Wingcase: Lemon wood
    duck

Originator: Cliff Zug
This excellent early-season nymph often is fished along weed beds, fairly deep. Try three or four, slow, short strips, then a longer retrieve. Stop, then repeat. It often works well in colder, early-spring water.

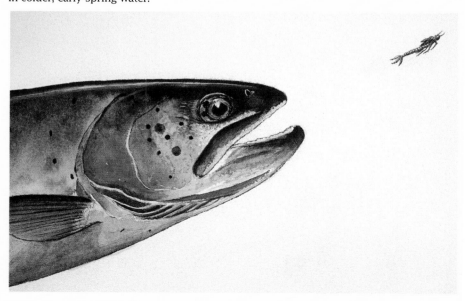

Miscellaneous Patterns

Northern Pike Fly

Hooks: #3/0, Salt
Thread: Fluorescent red
Tail: Saddle hackles
Head and Body: Rabbit fur strip

For the tail use matched sets of extra long, brightly colored saddle hackles: white/orange, white/red, orange/yellow, or red/yellow. Hackles should curve out, brighter colors on the outside. Toss this fly close to lily pads. Give it an erratic retrieve and hold on. Anglers travel hundreds of miles into northern Alberta and British Columbia to encounter the mighty northern pike. Increasing numbers of pike can now be found in Washington and Idaho waters.

Red and White Crappie Fly

Hooks: #4-8, Wet Fly
Thread: Black 3/0
Tail: Red fibers or hair
Body: Silver tinsel
Wing: White hair wing
Hackle: Soft red saddle
Eyes: Yellow and black enamel

Originator: Harry Faggetter, Spokane, Wash. This pattern was designed for crappie because they are attracted to red and white colors. They love it and so do many other species of fish, including perch.

Flies and Fly-fishing
for Steelhead

S ince the last edition of *Flies of the Northwest* was published in 1986, Western anadromous fisheries have deteriorated badly. In many cases, wild fish stocks have been depleted by habitat degradation and excessive harvest at sea and in rivers. In some cases, hatchery fish have helped fill in the gaps; in many situations they haven't. However, the future is not completely bleak, as increasing awareness of the problem is creating increased effort to save these splendid fish. The future of our steelhead fly-fishing lies in these efforts; we should all be part of them.

The last 10 years have also brought a continuing evolution in flies and fly-fishing for sea-run fish. This fly section includes a selection of patterns that are effective for the various sea-run fish. Some of these patterns are old friends that have been catching fish for a long time; others are recent creations that will someday become old favorites.

The last decade has brought a continuing evolution in steelhead flies. The traditional steelhead wet flies in vogue two decades ago are sharing popularity with flies incorporating flashy synthetic materials, in large part due to the effectiveness of these new patterns. At the same time, many steelheaders' preferences have reached back through time to continue the popularity of Spey patterns, Dee strip-wing patterns, and other modifications of old traditional Atlantic salmon flies. Surface flies have also continued to increase in popularity, and they're well represented here.

Fly tackle for steelhead has continued to improve and advance. Graphite rods have become even more efficient through the use of advanced-generation graphite fibers allowing more powerful rods to be constructed of ever lighter materials. At the same time, many steelheaders still enjoy the pleasure and feel of a traditional cane rod. Advanced graphite

Steelhead

also has allowed the surging popularity of two-handed rods for steelheading. Spey casting and longer overhead casting with such rods have permitted efficient access to drifts not generally available to the single-handed rod. Fly lines also have evolved with the major manufacturers now making steelhead tapers with longer bellies for better mending of long casts, Spey lines for the two-handed rods, and improved sinking and sink-tip lines.

The novice and expert both will find some productive flies in the following pages. For the novice, assembling a fly box for steelhead initially may seem difficult and confusing. One would still be wise to start with the basics—some traditional steelhead wet flies in size 4; consider a bright pattern such as the Comet or Fall Favorite, a contrast fly such as a Surgeon General, and a dark fly such as the Green Butt Skunk, a classic old standby. Add one of the dry/waking flies, a few of the flashy synthetic flies, a dark and a bright Spey pattern, and the novice has an excellent basic selection. Again, size 4 continues to be the most popular, but a few of the traditional wets should be tied in size 6 or 8, and some of the Spey patterns can be very effective in size 2 and 1 and even larger.

Fly-fishing for steelhead can roughly be divided into techniques for winter-run fish and for summer-run fish. Winter-run fish usually enter coastal rivers within several months of their late-winter or early-spring spawning time. Water temperatures are usually under 45° Fahrenheit and the fish tend to be less aggressive feeders.

Fishing techniques are aimed at bringing the fly down close to the fish. One of the most popular and effective methods involves using a high-density shooting head or a sink-tip line, quartering the cast upstream, and allowing the line and the fly to drift deeply through the holding water. Strike at any hesitation of the line. Leaders for this type of fishing should be short (one to three feet) to keep the fly down near the depth of the end of the fly line.

For both winter- and summer-run steelhead, many fly fishers use floating lines with long leaders and a weighted fly or a split shot six to eight inches above the fly. This technique is much the same as that used when nymph fishing for trout. The angler works close to the holding water, then casts quartering upstream above the expected holding water. The angler allows the fly to drift downstream, mending the line to keep a deep, free drift of the fly. Strike at any hesitation of the line. Strike indicators might help detect some subtle strikes. This technique will work well with virtually any steelhead fly, but many anglers use an egg pattern in the winter or spring, or a dark stonefly nymph anytime. This floating line, deep-drift method is very effective, and is gaining in popularity.

Summer-run steelhead generally enter freshwater five to 12 months before their spring spawning time. When they first enter rivers, water temperatures are usually above 45° Fahrenheit, and frequently above 60° in summer. These are often fish of large inland river systems, although many coastal rivers have summer runs as well as winter runs.

Most summer-run steelheaders use sink-tip or floating lines with wet flies. Casts are made quartering downstream, allowing the fly to sweep across the current. The line should be mended upstream or away from the shore to slow the rate of movement of the fly across the current. The faster the flow, the more frequently the mends should be made to keep the fly from "whipping" across the current. Be sure to allow the fly to hang for a few seconds straight below your casting position at the end of the swing. Steelhead apparently follow a fly across the currents to take it when it straightens out and stops at the end of the drift. Aggressive summer-run fish striking against the tight line usually hook themselves in the corner of the jaw as they turn away to return to their lie. The strike will be more than obvious to the angler, who needs only to raise the rod and keep the line tight to the fish. Keep your hands off the reel and line initially, as it is easy to break fish off by overreacting to the surging strike.

Leaders on sink-tip lines are usually three to five feet long, and for floating lines, eight to ten feet. Tippet strengths of eight to 10 pounds are commonly used, but in clear small rivers six-pound tippet might be more effective. Six-pound tippet is the lightest that should be used for these fish because of the hard strikes and the need to aggressively play the fish to keep from exhausting them. The fly fisher wants to make a safe, quick release.

Fishing for steelhead on the surface continues to increase in popularity. Some steelhead can be caught on dead-drifted, bushy dry flies, but more fish are likely to be attracted to a fly skimming or skating across the surface. This can be done by riffle hitching a standard wet-fly so that it skims on the surface film, but is probably more effective with flies designed for surface fishing, such as a Grease Liner, Riffle Dancer, Waller Waker, or Bomber. These flies will stay on the surface while free-drifting or while tensioned against the line on a downstream cast. The latter technique is much the same as dry-line, wet-fly fishing, with casts made quartering downstream. Upstream or downstream mends may be necessary to keep the fly waking on the surface. The primary difference in this method is the need to allow fish to suck the fly into their mouth if they don't outright gulp it. This can be done by either fishing with the rod tip up and dropping it at the first sign of a strike, or by keeping the rod low and holding a 12- to 18-inch loop of line under the rod-hand index finger and releasing the loop at the first sign of a strike. With either method, don't raise the rod until the line is pulled tight by the fish.

Surface fly-fishing for steelhead is truly exciting, especially since a fish may play with the fly on several casts before finally taking it or leaving it!

A number of fine books are available to further your knowledge about steelhead fly-fishing. Recommended references include *Steelhead Fly-fishing*, by Trey Combs, *Advanced Fly Fishing for Steelhead*, by Deke Meyer, and *Dry Line Steelhead Fishing*, by Bill McMillan.

Steelhead

Blue Charm (Western Tie)

Hook: #2-6, STLHD
Thread: Black 3/0
Tail: Golden pheasant
Rib: Silver tinsel
Body: Black floss
Wing: Bronze mallard
Hackle: Blue saddle
Topping: Pheasant crest

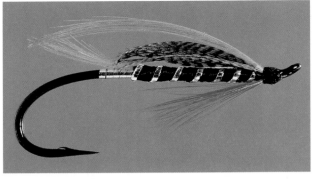

This pattern is adapted from a well-known British salmon fly for use as a western steelhead fly. The pattern is usually tied low-water style on fine wire hooks and proportioned two sizes smaller than normal for the hook. Low-water style flies are most commonly used for summer-run steelhead in clear water.

Boss

Hook: #2-6, STLHD
Thread: Black 3/0
Tail: Black bucktail
Rib: Silver tinsel
Body: Black chenille
Hackle: Orange saddle
Eyes: Bead chain

Originator: Virgil Sullivan, Forestville, Calif.
The Boss is the most common variation of the Comet series of steelhead patterns. Bead chain or lead eyes are added, depending on water depth and speed, so that the fly can be fished close to the bottom.

Comet

Hook: #1/0-8, STLHD
Thread: Black 3/0
Tail: Orange bucktail
Body: Silver oval tinsel
Hackle: Orange saddle

Originator: Howard Norton, Sebastopol, Calif.
An excellent fly for winter-run steelhead. First developed in the 1940s, it came into its own during the 1950s. This pattern may be tied with bead chain or lead eyes which allows it to be fished at greater depths. Various color combinations are also popular. The tail is tied at least as long as the body.

Fall Favorite
Hook: #2-6, STLHD
Thread: Black 3/0
Body: Silver tinsel
Hackle: Red saddle
Wing: Orange bucktail

This fly was originated in California during the 1940s for use on the Eel River. Tied in fluorescent colors it is a standard for winter-run steelhead from California to Canada. Shown tied in low-water style.

Freight Train
Hook: #2/0-8, STLHD
Thread: Black 3/0
Tail: Purple hackle fibers
Rib: Silver oval tinsel, fine
Butt: Orange and red floss
Body: Black chenille
Hackle: Purple saddle
Wing: White calf tail

Originator: Randall Kaufmann, Portland, Ore. This top-producing fly on Oregon's Deschutes River is really a Skunk variation. The black body/white wing combination provides the alternate contrast in color that is probably the basis of the effectiveness of both the Skunk and Freight Train. The bright orange and red double butt with purple hackle and tail add popular steelhead colors to this fly.

Kalama Special
Hook: #4-8, STLHD
Thread: Black 3/0
Tail: Red hackle
Rib: Golden badger hackle
Body: Yellow wool
Wing: White bucktail

Originator: Mike Kennedy, Oswego, Ore.
Although this fly is named for the Kalama River in southwestern Washington, it has proven very effective for steelhead on inland rivers. A popular variation substitutes red polypropylene for the yellow body shown.

Steelhead

Purple Peril
Hook: #4-8, STLHD
Thread: Black 3/0
Tag: Silver flat tinsel
Tail: Purple hackle fibers
Rib: Silver oval tinsel
Body: Purple floss
Hackle: Purple saddle
Wing: Deer hair

Originator: Ken McLeod, Seattle, Wash.
This fly was introduced in the late 1930s and has been a standard for more than 40 years. Purple chenille may be substituted for the body. Purple is a highly visible color in most light conditions, making this fly pattern very effective for summer- and winter-run steelhead.

Skunk, Green Butt
Hook: #1-10, STLHD
Thread: Black 3/0
Tail: Red hackle
Rib: Silver tinsel
Body: Black and green chenille
Hackle: Black saddle
Wing: White bucktail

Originators: Wes Drain, Seattle, Wash., and Mildred Krogel, Roseburg, Ore.
The Skunk is probably the most popular steelhead pattern in the Northwest today. Effective variations include the addition of red

or green butt to the black body and jungle cock feathers to the cheeks. The Skunk first appeared in the late 1930s and has provided numerous steelhead for beginner and experienced fly fishers ever since.

Skykomish Sunrise
Hook: #2-8, STLHD
Thread: Black 3/0
Tail: Red and yellow hackle
Rib: Silver tinsel oval
Body: Red fur
Hackle: Red and yellow saddle
Wing: White bucktail

Originators: Ken and George McLeod, Seattle, Wash.
This pattern was inspired by a sunrise on the Skykomish River in Washington state about 1940. It has become a standard steelhead pattern taking many record-sized fish on the Kispiox River including a 29-pound 2-ounce steelhead by George McLeod in 1955. The fly pictured is tied sparse in a low-water style. This pattern traditionally is tied as a winter-run fly with a much heavier body and wing.

Surgeon General
Hook: #2-10, STLHD
Thread: Black 3/0
Tail: Red hackle
Tag and Rib: Silver wire
Body: Purple wool
Hackle: Red
Wing: White bucktail

Originator: Del O. Cooper, Portland, Ore.

Like the Skunk, this fly incorporates a highly visible contrasting white wing and dark body and adds purple and red attractor colors producing a

beautiful fly. Although it is considered a steelhead pattern, it is also effective for sea-run cutthroat.

Bomber
Hook: #2-6, STLHD
Thread: Black multi-strand
Tail: White calf tail
Hackle: Grizzly palmered
Body: Deer hair
Wing: White calf tail

Originator: Rev. Elmer L. Smith, New Brunswick, Canada

An excellent skating fly in all speeds of water. Originally designed for Atlantic salmon, it has adapted well for steelhead in Western rivers. It is often used as a searching pattern for occasional steelhead in large waters. The only drawback when using a skating fly is the need to pause and allow the fish to suck the fly into its mouth after the surging surface strike. The calf-tail wing is tied forward.

Grease Liner
Hook: #2-8, STLHD, 1XF
Thread: Black Nymo, size A
Tail: Fine deer body hair
Body: Black dubbing
Hackle: Grizzly, sparse
Wing: Deer body hair

Originator: Harry Lemire, Black Diamond, Wash.

This pattern was developed in 1962 and presented as a dry-fly or a skating, waking fly. The body is the same length as the tail and is colored

to match the egg-laying caddisflies found in the stream fished. Brown, green, and orange body colors are popular variations.

Riffle Dancer
Hook: #2-4, STLHD
Thread: Brown monocord 3/0
Tail: Deer hair
Rib: Overwrapped tying thread
Body: Deer hair
Wing: Deer hair

Originator: Mark Pinch, Spokane, Wash.
This pattern is a waking fly that will skitter across fast or slow water. It has proven itself throughout the inland Northwest, and has had excellent success in the Skeena River system in B.C. The fly has the front 1/3 of the hook shank bent up about 30 degrees. Do this after the fly is tied, it will flair the wings and collar properly. It skitters most actively when riffle-hitched around the throat.

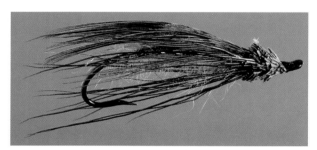

Thompson River Caddis
Hook: #2-6, STLHD
Thread: Black 6/0
Rib: Black 6/0
Body: Insect green dubbing
Wing: Green phase pheasant rump
Head: Moose body hair

Originator: Harry Lemire, Black Diamond, Wash.

This low-water pattern is a simple-to-tie caddis imitation. It is fished with greased-line technique, but without the Portland (riffle) hitch. This allows the fly to mix in the surface film and present a more visible silhouette to underlying steelhead. The spun moose-hair head is clipped flat on top and bottom and cemented to keep its shape.

Waller Waker
Hook: #2-6, STLHD
Thread: Black multi-strand
Tail: Dark moose or elk hair
Body: Brown and black deer hair
Wing: Elk hair
Throat: Dark moose or elk hair

Originator: Lani Waller, Novato, Calif.
This skittering surface fly was developed by Lani Waller to entice steelhead to the surface. The throat acts as a rudder, which enables the fly to skate across the surface of the water on a downstream swing. Many steelheaders are using waking flies to help spot resting fish. If the steelhead is not hooked with the dry-fly, it can often be taken by switching to a sub-surface fly.

Western Steelhead Bee

Hook: #2/0-6, STLHD
Thread: Black monocord
Tail: Red fox squirrel
Body: Yellow and brown deer
Wing: Red fox squirrel tail
Hackle: Brown, four feathers

Originator: Roderick Haig-Brown, Vancouver, British Columbia

One of the oldest dry-fly steelhead patterns, fished dead-drift or skated. Brown and yellow wool may be substituted for deer hair for forming body. Deer hair makes the fly more buoyant, which enhances its skating characteristics especially in fast, heavy water. The squirrel-tail wing is tied forward and divided.

After Dinner Mint

Hook: #2-6, Wet Fly, 3XL
Thread: Black mono 3/0
Body: Green poly flash
Wing: See text
Head: Black deer hair spun

Originator: Mark Noble, Vancouver, Wash.

Mark has had success using Muddler-style heads on steelhead patterns since the late 1970s. This pattern has become a standard for southwestern Washington steelheaders. Smaller versions work well in Western streams which hold large trout. The wing is pearl Krystal Flash under purple squirrel tail, under black marabou.

Deschutes Special

Hook: #2-6, STLHD
Thread: Red 6/0
Rib: Gold Diamond Braid
Body: Red Uni-Floss
Wing: White bucktail
Beard: Purple saddle

This pattern incorporates ideas from several different successful Deschutes River steelhead flies. It is simple to tie, rugged, and fishes well not only on the Deschutes River but on most other Pacific Northwest steelhead rivers. Also tied with silver Diamond Braid rib and dark blue beard. Pearl Krystal Flash highlights the wing.

Steelhead

Egg Sucking Leech
Hook: #1-6, STLHD
Thread: Black 6/0
Tail: Black marabou
Hackle: Black, palmered
Body: Black chenille
Head: Red-orange chenille

Originating as an Alaskan rainbow fly, this pattern has proven itself as a superb steelhead fly as well as for coho salmon. A purple variation is popular in Skeena River tributaries. Can be fished un-weighted on floating lines, but is probably more effective on sink-tip lines with the front 1/3 of the hook weighted. Colored bead heads and the addition of a few strands of Krystal Flash in the tail are popular variations.

Flashdancer
Hook: #2/0-4, STLHD
Thread: Black 3/0
Body: Pearl braided Mylar
Wing: Krystal Flash and orange marabou
Head: Bead eyes

Originator: Charles Smith, Tri-Cities, Wash.
This flashy fly has proven quite successful in the Ringold Springs area of the Columbia River Reach near Hanford, Wash., as well as other Northwest steelhead waters. Charles Smith developed it in 1993. The wing is red and silver Krystal Flash topped by long orange marabou.

Kaleidoscope
Hook: #2-6, STLHD
Thread: Black 6/0
Tail: Red-orange hackle fibers
Underbody: Purple floss
Body: Pearl Flashabou
Hackle: Blue and purple saddle
Wing: Calf tail, Krystal Flash
Overwing: Orange marabou

Originator: Walt Balek, Spokane, Wash.
As water temperatures drop, this pattern moves steelhead well in both traditional runs and faster pocket water. The floss and single wrap pearlescent Flashabou body glows like a neon light, even on cloudy days. The wing is layered white calf tail under pearlescent Krystal Flash under blue/purple Flashabou. The body is often counterwrapped with fine gold wire.

Max Flash
Hook: #2-6, STLHD
Thread: Black 3/0
Tail: Orange hackle fibers
Rib: Silver wire, fine
Body: Purple Flashabou, wrapped
Wing: Krystal Flash and marabou
Hackle: Purple Schlappen

Originator: Randy Shaber,
Spokane, Wash.
This pattern combines the movement of marabou and the sparkle
of Krystal Flash. The dark silhouette and flashy underbody produce
strikes throughout the day. Heavily
dressed large sizes are best when
visibility is impaired by water

clarity or low light. The wing is tied with pearl and pink Krystal Flash under pink and purple marabou under blue Krystal Flash. Also tied with orange and black wings.

Mi-Tie
Hook: #6-8, SALT
Head: Brass bead
Thread: Orange 3/0
Tail: Brown bucktail
Body: Hot orange floss
Hackle: Orange saddle palmered

Originator: Dennis Evans,
Toppenish, Wash.
This small fly has proven to be an
exceptional producer for steelhead in tributary river mouths
along the Columbia River. It is
fished with long leaders using
wet-cell shooting heads or No. 2 sinking lines in water less than 20 feet deep. Use a slow
retrieve and fish near the bottom in stillwaters. Black and purple are also effective colors.
The tail should be at least twice the body length.

Orange and Black
Hook: #1/0-4, STLHD
Thread: Black Multi-Strand
Tag: Gold tinsel
Rib: Gold oval tinsel, medium
Body: Black tying thread
Wing: See text
Beard: Orange polar bear

Originator: Jake Gahlke,
Orofino, Ida.
Jake fishes most days of the
fall season and this pattern is

his all-time favorite. It is a consistent producer fished grease line or sink-tip. Jake's fly has
been successful throughout the Northwest and Canada. The wing is built (bottom to top)
with orange polar bear, orange Krystal Flash, bright orange marabou, and red golden
pheasant body feather.

Steelhead

Orange Beauty

Hook: #4, STLHD
Thread: Fluorescent orange 3/0
Hackle: Orange saddle hackle
Body: Orange Edge Bright and tinsel
Wing: Pearl Krystal Flash

Originator: Loyd Bibbee, Spokane, Wash.
This bright fly has proved effective in steelhead rivers in both Canada and the United States. Various color

combinations of hackle and Edge Bright strips wrapped over flat silver tinsel work well.

Squamish Poacher

Hook: #2-6, Wet Fly
Thread: Orange 6/0
Feelers: Orange bucktail
Eyes: Glass on mono
Hackle: Orange, palmered
Body: Orange chenille
Shell: Orange surveyor's tape

Originator: Joe Kembietz, Vancouver, B.C.
Used on coastal rivers for winter-run steelhead, presented as a realistic shrimp pattern. This fly is a favorite of Canadian steelheaders, and it is often fished weighted. Eyes are made by melting a bead on one end of monofilament, stringing two glass beads and melting a bead on other end.

Fancy Spade

Hook: #2-4, STLHD
Thread: Red 3/0
Tail: Deer hair
Body: Peacock herl and black ostrich
Hackle: Grizzly

Originator: Alec Jackson, Kenmore, Wash.
Alec Jackson feels his Spade series is as effective as Skunk patterns because of the contrasting dark body, light wing concept. Make ropes of peacock herl and ostrich herl

with oval tinsel before wrapping as body. Wrap rear half of body with peacock herl rope, and taper front half with black ostrich herl rope as shown.

Red Guina (Pseudo Spey)
Hook: #1-4, STLHD
Thread: Red 6/0
Rear Body: Red floss
Front Body: Claret dubbing
Hackle: Red guinea and red neck

Originator: Alec Jackson, Kenmore, Wash.

This durable steelhead pattern is tied "in the round" style, and presents the same profile from all angles. The soft hackle pulses and breathes in even light currents. This pattern is tied in a variety of light and dark colors. The floss and dubbing material of the body are protected by twisting each with fine silver wire before wrapping onto the hook.

Steelhead Woolie
Hook: #2, STLHD
Thread: Black 6/0
Tag and Rib: Silver tinsel
Body: Black Cactus Chenille
Hackle: Blue-eared pheasant

Originator: Dave Gunderson, Spokane, Wash.

An excellent dark-day fly which fishes well in slow-moving water and riffle areas too. The long, black, blue-eared pheasant fibers react to the slightest current and entice steelhead to the natural pulsating motion. Large peacock breast feathers are often substituted for the blue-eared pheasant. Various bright body colors work well during midday periods. Another variation includes a grizzly hackle, palmered over the body.

Blue Drain
Hook: #3, STLHD
Thread: Black 6/0
Body: Blue Diamond Braid
Hackle: Blue saddle palmered
Collar: Mallard flank
Wing: Polar bear over flash

Originator: Tom Darling, Seattle, Wash.

This fly was designed as a tribute to the late Wes Drain, avid steelheader and outdoor writer. It works best for spring-, fall- and winter-run steelhead in most Puget Sound drainages. Various color combinations work well including red and purple. Arctic fox can be substituted for polar bear and mixed with various colors of Krystal Flash.

Steelhead

Cerise/Claret Spey

Hook: #2-4, STLHD
Thread: Red monocord
Tag: Silver embossed tinsel
Rib: Silver oval tinsel
Body: Claret wool and Spey
  feather
Hackle: Mallard flank

Originator: John Newbury, Chewelah, Wash.
This classic Spey-style pattern is tied with eye-catching bright colored and variegated hackles. The pulsating hackled silhouette partly conceals its long flashy tinsel tag, tempting wary steelhead to strike. Spey feather is a bleached goose shoulder feather dyed cerise. The hackle is natural over claret-dyed mallard flank.

Coast Orange

Hook: #2/0-4, STLHD
Thread: Burgundy 6/0
Tail: Red golden pheasant
Rib: Wire over pearl Mylar
Body: Orange fur
Wing: Orange calf tail and
  hackle
Hackle: Red golden pheasant

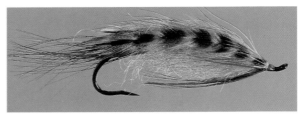

Originator: Dec Hogan, Mt. Vernon, Wash.
This fly fishes best when weighted slightly at the head of hook. This easily tied Spey style pattern was originated to imitate shrimp for use on coastal rivers for steelhead. Many color combinations also work well and produce savage strikes.

Heavy Breather Orange

Hook: #2/0-4, STLHD
Thread: Orange 6/0
Tag: Gold flat tinsel
Rib: Gold fine oval tinsel
Body: Orange floss and fur
Wing: Orange grizzly
  hackle
Hackle: Orange Spey, and
  teal

Originator: Harry Dritz, Vancouver, Wash.
The Heavy Breather works well on the Kalama River in the fall and is generally a good winter fly. Dark purple versions are also effective. Flat tinsel is wrapped over the entire hook shank, then overlain with floss, giving added brightness to the body. Strip one side of the Spey hackle for easier wrapping. Tie in Spey feather by tip before dubbing fur body.

Marabou Spey

Hook: #3/0-2, STLHD
Thread: Red multi strand 3/0
Body: Purple marabou plumes
Hackle: Cerise marabou
    plume

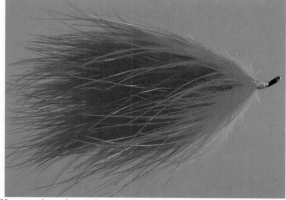

Originator: Gordon Olson,
Spokane, Wash.

A simple but very effective fly for both steelhead and salmon. Three marabou plumes are tied in by the tip then wound around the shank of hook, Spey style, stroking the fibers toward rear of hook. Several color combinations are effective, but this color combination works well in all water clarity conditions and daylight periods.

Psycho Shrimp

Hook: #2/0-2, STLHD
Thread: Burgundy 6/0
Feelers: Orange squirrel
Eyes: Mono bead
Body: See text

Originator: Dec Hogan,
Mt. Vernon, Wash.

This pattern, a take-off of the General Practitioner, is very effective in coastal rivers for winter- and spring-run steelhead. Fishing guide Dec Hogan prefers an orange pattern, but black, purple, and olive are also effective. The body is produced with hot orange dubbing separated into four segments by 2-3 turns of orange-dyed pheasant rump feathers at each segment. Two golden pheasant neck feathers are tied in flat over each segment, as shown.

The Gardener

Hook: #1/0-4, STLHD
Thread: Black 3/0
Tags: Oval gold tinsel, floss
Tail: Golden pheasant
Rib: Oval over flat silver tinsel
Body: Yellow, green and blue
    fur
Spey Hackle: Long black
Wing: Brown squirrel tail

Mr. Garden originated this fly in the mid-nineteenth century, thus the name Gardener. This Dee strip-wing variation uses squirrel tail in the wing. Obtainable materials have been substituted for the seal fur and heron called for in the original pattern. Harry Lemire submitted this complex, but beautiful westernized Atlantic style pattern to present some classic options to Western steelheaders. Jungle cock at cheeks is optional. The tail includes both crest and tippet feathers.

Steelhead

The Tartan
Hook: #1/0-4, STLHD
Thread: Black 3/0
Tag: Gold flat tinsel
Tail: Golden pheasant rump
Rib: Gold oval tinsel
Body: Orange, then scarlet fur
Spey Hackle: Badger and teal
Wing: Gray squirrel

This is another Westernized Atlantic salmon pattern submitted by Harry Lemire.
This fly was originated in the mid-eighteenth century. Harry has substituted body and wing materials from the original, but the rich history of Atlantic salmon patterns is still evident in this fly. Harry maintains "Antiques can still catch fish!" The body material is seal fur substitute, and the squirrel tail wing is tied low and divided.

GELORENSON

Saltwater Fly-fishing

*M*any favorite lakes and streams in the Northwest are being overburdened by a relent-lessly growing number of new fly fishers. There is, however, challenging, uncrowded fly-fishing available to the angler willing to forsake the confines and comfort zone of a stream or pond and explore saltwater.

Most Western anglers who fish for bass or steelhead already have most of the tackle required to fish in the salt: a 7- or 8-weight rod, a large capacity reel, and a sink-tip or sink-ing fly line.

Over the past several years, saltwater fly-fishing has gained its own following of devotees, most of whom cut their teeth on trout fishing in freshwater. Unfortunately, the saltwater fly-fishing places that grab most of the press are toney and pricey venues like Belize, Costa Rica, or Christmas Island, but you don't have to travel to an exotic, faraway destination to find great saltwater fly-fishing.

The Pacific Coast from California to Alaska is loaded with places to unlimber a fly rod. Some of the most productive saltwater fly-fishing near home is on the protected waters of Washington's Puget Sound and the beaches of Vancouver Island in British Columbia. Somewhat more remote are the countless estuaries along the Tongass National Forest in southeast Alaska. Even in these days of depressed fish stocks, the Pacific Ocean and its estuaries still hold good populations of rockfish, albacore, bonito, striped bass, five species of salmon, sea-run cutthroat, Dolly Varden ,and a long list of other finny critters.

For tying saltwater flies, high-tech, synthetic materials hang on fly shop pegs, begging to be turned into anchovy, herring, sand lance, sardine, sculpin, and shrimp imitations. The saltwater tier has unrestricted room to experiment, blending a montage of synthetic

Saltwater Fly-fishing

materials into new patterns ranging from bulky, five-inch baitfish to size 14 sparsely dressed shrimp.

New saltwater anglers may be surprised to discover that the smallest bonito, surf perch, coho salmon, or sea-run cutthroat hooked in the salt will pull every bit as hard as the largest trout taken in a favorite stream or lake. Make sure your tackle is properly assembled, because any saltwater fish over three pounds is going to test the integrity of your backing splice.

Many of the patterns listed in the sea-run cutthroat and salmon chapters are excellent all-purpose saltwater flies which will attract a variety of game fish..

Beach Bug
Hook: #6-8, STLHD
Thread: Gray or black 6/0
Tail: Long guinea, 6-8 fibers
Body: Blue dun hare's ear
Eyes: Black mono, medium
Wing: Pheasant rump

Originator: Eric Balser, Mount Vernon, Wash.
This fly was developed to imitate the small inshore shrimps and crab larvae found in the intertidal zone of Puget Sound beaches. Sea-run cutthroat, Dollies, young salmon, and all varieties of shallow-water bottom fish respond well to this fly. Walk the beach with a floating line as the fly drifts with the tide. Sharp rhythmic twitches sometimes help if the current is slow.

Musselbed Mino
Hook: #4-8, SALT
Thread: Light gray 6/0
Body: Pearl Diamond Braid
Eyes: Dumbbell
Throat: Gray marabou tips
Wing: Bucktail

Originator: Eric Balser, Mount Vernon, Wash.

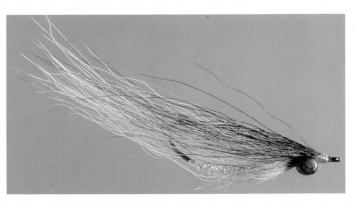

An all-purpose minnow imitation. Because of its keel design this fly can be worked directly on the bottom, if desired, for sea-run cutthroat and Dollies on Puget Sound beaches. The weighted versions seem to keel best, even during a fast retrieve, and can be worked deeply even with a floating line. The wing can be tied with layers of gray, olive, and brown bucktail or marabou.

Saltwater and Freshwater Fly-fishing for Salmon

*A*ll five species of Pacific salmon are exciting quarry for the Northwest fly fisher, and more and more fly anglers are fishing for them. With the exception of chinook salmon, Pacific salmon can be pursued effectively in saltwater by locating feeding fish or by fishing for them in pre-spawning staging areas near the mouths of streams. More fly fishers fish for them after they've entered the streams on their spawning runs, as they are more concentrated and reachable with fly-fishing methods in streams than they are while they're still in saltwater.

Fly tackle commonly used for chum, sockeye, and coho (silver) salmon includes 7-, 8-, and 9-weight systems: for chinook (king) salmon, 9 and 10 weight systems; and for the smaller pink (humpy) salmon, 5 to 8 weight systems. In all cases, reels should have smooth drags and hold at least 100 yards of backing. Leaders and tippets for all of the larger salmon should be on the stout side, 10 to 15 pounds—and even stronger for big chinooks.

Fishing for salmon in saltwater frequently requires long casts and deep presentations to reach fish; high-density shooting heads are commonly used, although there are times when sink-tip and even floating lines may be effective. Flies usually imitate prey, and the Tri-color Streamer and Ferguson's Green and Silver are good examples of the type of fly used. The flies are actively retrieved with rapid strips of the line to imitate the movement of a fleeing baitfish.

In saltwater, locating salmon is obviously the key to catching them, and several books that deal specifically with fishing for salmon in the salt are mentioned at the end of this section. In freshwater, salmon can be easier to locate, especially where it's shallow water. Chums and sockeyes usually move and hold in shallow water over gravel bars. Coho and

Salmon

humpies frequently school in backwaters and flows of moderate depth. Chinook will typically hold in deep runs and pools until they are on their spawning beds. In rivers, all are susceptible to attractor patterns such as the Silver Autumn, Cactus Buggers, and various egg flies.

Salmon in rivers may take the fly drifted at a constant speed, but often seem more willing to strike a fly that is being retrieved in front of them. Egg patterns, of course, should be dead-drifted with the current along the bottom.

Some fly fishers pursue Pacific salmon, primarily humpies, chums, and coho, in rivers with surface flies. The bright Wog, or Pink Polliwog, is one such fly. It helps to fish it over a concentration of holding fish because only a relatively small percentage of fish in a pod will take a fly on the surface. The technique is much like skating steelhead flies on the surface, except that salmon seem more prone to chase a fly that is being retrieved in 8- to 12-inch strips.

Also, your success is likely to be better in water three feet deep or less. Slashing strikes may come from nowhere, but commonly a wake will appear behind the fly as a salmon stalks it. Salmon sometimes just nip at the fly without actually taking it, so it usually best to delay striking until you feel the weight of the fish against the line.

Obviously, fly-fishing for Pacific salmon can offer tremendous thrills. To learn more about fly-fishing for Pacific salmon, refer to the excellent book *Fly Fishing for Pacific Salmon*, by Bruce Ferguson, Les Johnson, and Pat Trotter. Two new works have just been published on fly-fishing for salmon in saltwater, *Saltwater Fly-fishing for Pacific Salmon*, by Barry Thornton, and *Salmon To a Fly*, by Jim Crawford.

Pixie Revenge
Hook: #2/0-4, STLHD
Thread: Red 3/0
Body: White and orange
   marabou
Collar: Cerise marabou

Originator: George Cook, Tigard, Ore.
This marabou fly represents an Alaskan series of flies tied in various color combinations to fish for steelhead and salmon. Additional marabou colors include green, black, yellow, purple, and blue. Various colors of Mylar and Krystal Flash are added throughout the marabou. Dark body and bright collar combinations work well in "dirty" water.

Egg
Hook: #4-8, Egg
Thread: Hot pink 3/0
Body: Clipped egg yarn

Various egg style patterns in different sizes and colors are very effective for salmon, steelhead and large trout in many rivers throughout the West, Canada and Alaska. Pom-poms found in craft stores can be substituted for the clipped Glo-Bug yarn. Scud hooks are also commonly used.

Cactus Bugger
Hook: #1-4, STLHD
Thread: Red 6/0
Tail: Red over pink
   marabou
Body: Pink Cactus
   Chenille
Hackle: Red

Popularized in Alaska, it is simply outstanding for salmon in freshwater, particularly coho and chinook. In sizes 4 and 6 it is an excellent steelhead fly. It can be tied in other color variations: black, purple, and blue combinations are excellent for steelhead. International guide Frans Jansen ties it with dumbbell eyes made of split shot on a loop of mono to use in backwaters for coho salmon. Flashabou is sometimes added to the tail.

Salmon

Silver Autumn
Hook: #2-4, STLHD
Thread: Yellow monocord
Tail: Pink and yellow buck-
tail
Tag and Body: Braided pearl
Mylar
Wing: Same as tail
Overwing: Gold Flashabou
Hackle: Orange Schlappen

Originator: Ed Ward
Alaskan guide Ed Ward has
developed many productive
patterns for salmon, steel-
head, and trout. This pattern is a top producer for coho salmon and also is useful for
steelhead. It fishes well on the swing, strip, or dead-drift with intermittent twitches.

Salt–Freshwater Streamer
Hook: #4/0-4, SALT
Thread: Black monocord
Wing: Bucktail Krystal
Flash
Throat: White marabou
Eyes: Painted or doll
eyes

Originator: Gene
Lorenson, Spokane,
Wash.
This minnow imitation
can be used for a variety
of saltwater species,
including salmon, and works well in freshwater for trout and grayling. The wing material is
stacked with light on the bottom to dark on top. Color combinations include yellow, chartreuse, and light blue, and green, dark green, blue, and purple. Black forms the topmost
centerline stripe. Large eyes are attractive and dumbbell eyes may be used for weighted
versions.

Wog
Hook: #1 1/2-3,
STLHD
Thread: Pink mono-
cord
Wing: Pink marabou
over Flashabou
Head: Pink deer hair

Originator: Dec
Hogan, Mount
Vernon, Wash., and
Ed Ward
This pattern was developed to attract salmon to surface flies. It has proven to be highly
effective for most salmon, and also works for steelhead, bass, and pike. It's productive on
the swing, strip, and dead-drift. Pink, silver, or blue Flashabou may be used.

Green and Silver

Hook: #2-4, SALT, long
Thread: Black 3/0
Tail: White hair and pearl flash
Body: Silver Braid and chenille
Wing: Same as tail
Topping: Pearl crystal hair
Head: Black tying thread

Originator: Bruce M. Ferguson, Gig Harbor, Wash.

This is Bruce Ferguson's favorite fly for feeding coho throughout the Puget Sound and Canadian waters around the Queen Charlotte and Vancouver Island areas. It is most effective with a fast, erratic stripping action on a full-sinking, intermediate, or sink-tip line. Size 4 works best for salmon, and smaller sizes work well for Belize bonefish. Body is Diamond Braid and chartreuse chenille.

Patterns for Non–feeding Mature Salmon

Humpy Fly

Hook: #2-8, SALT
Thread: Black 6/0
Body: Silver Mylar tinsel
Wing: Super Hair and Krystal Flash
Eyes: Small silver bead chain

Originator: Bill Ackerlund
This is a proven pattern for pink salmon, which are com-

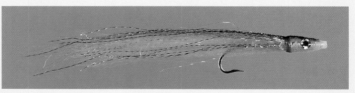

monly called humpies because of the hump that appears on the backs of spawning males. It is very effective from Washington to Alaska, from estuaries to upper river pools. A few strands of pearl Krystal Flash are enclosed between white and pink Super Hair wing segments. Additional colors: Bright green over white, blue over white, and black over white.

Puget Sound Sand Lance

Hook: #2, SALT
Tubing: 1/8" and 3/16" I.D. tubing
Thread: White and clear mono
Underbody: White floss and Super Hair
Blood Line: Pink Super Hair
Underwing: Gray Super Hair
Midwing: Olive Super Hair
Topwing: Black Krystal Flash

Median Line: Silver Krystal Flash
Gills: Red thread, or marking pen
Head: 5-minute epoxy, tubes
Eyes: Witchcraft, silver stick-on

Originator: Les Johnson, Seattle, Wash.
This pattern is time-consuming to tie, but is nearly indestructible and the hook is easily replaced. The fly in 2 1/2- to 4-inch lengths is deadly for most salmon, and smaller sizes will take cutthroat along Puget Sound beaches. Super Hair coloration in wing can be varied with gray, bright green, and blue combinations.

Fly-fishing for Sea-run Cutthroat

S ea-run cutthroat seem to be designed for the fly fisher. They commonly feed on smaller organisms best imitated with a fly. When in saltwater, they frequently remain in estuaries and intertidal areas near the mouths of their native rivers, where fly fishers find them. They typically start their upstream migration in late summer or early fall, hence their name "harvest trout." Spawning takes place in late winter, and may occur well up in the smaller tributaries of the river systems. These fish take their time on the upstream run, and are available to the river fly angler for a good portion of the year.

Fly tackle in 4- to 7-weight systems work well. Sink-tip lines are often useful, but since these fish retain the cutthroat family tendency to feed at or near the surface, floating lines can frequently be used. Leaders are much the same as for other trout fishing, with tippets of 3- to 6-pound strength employed.

Sea-run cutthroat fishing often involves fishing near underwater structures. In estuaries the fish hang out around points and coves, near jetties, pilings, and rock piles. Flies that work well in these areas include small baitfish patterns and imitative patterns such as the Beach Bug and Musselbed Minnow. In rivers, sea-run cutthroat revert quickly to trout feeding behavior, but their lies are still commonly structure-related: boulder-strewn pools, log jams, and cutbanks. Standard match-the-hatch fishing can work, but these fish are very susceptible to attractor patterns, such as the Bucktail Coachman, Dark Spruce, and Muddler Minnow.

A fine book, *How to Fish for Sea-Run Cutthroat Trout*, by Les Johnson, will further your knowledge about this fish.

Sea-run Cutthroat and Other Estuary Patterns

Thorne River Emerger

Hooks: #4-8, SALT long
Thread: Black 6/0
Body: Silver Mylar tinsel
Wing: Super Hair
Mid-line: Silver Krystal Flash
Topping: Green peacock herl

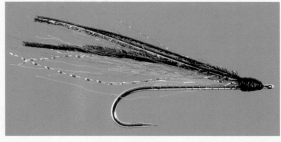

Originators: Les Johnson and
Dan Lemaich, Seattle, Wash.
This fly was created on Prince
of Wales Island to imitate pink and chum fry heading down the Thorne River in the spring.
It's a deadly producer on coastal cutthroat and Dolly Varden and also is an excellent imitation of the small sand lance that hatch along the beaches of Puget Sound. The tinsel body
is double wrapped and lacquered. The wing should be tied sparse with layers of olive, pink,
and white Super Hair.

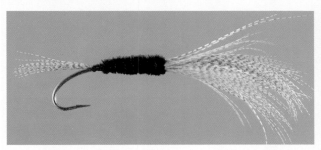

Reverse Spider

Hook: #4-8, SALT long
Thread: Black 3/0
Tail: Mallard
Wing: Mallard
Body: Black chenille

Originator: Mike Kinney
Arlington, Wash.
The Reverse Spider was
designed for Stilla-
guamish sea-run cutthroat about 1975. The reverse, forward-tied wing produces an incred-
ible undulating motion when retrieved. It will draw strikes from sea-run cutthroat and Dolly
Varden when other patterns don't. The chenille body is double wrapped over the tied-in
butts of the tail and wing. Alternative colors include red and yellow for the body and
yellow wings. Wet fly hooks may be used, but need to be rinsed after use.

Silver Brown

Hook: 2-8, STLHD
Thread: Black 3/0
Tail: Imitation Indian Crow
Body: Silver Mylar tinsel
Hackle: Golden pheasant
    flank
Underwing: Orange calf tail
Overwing: Golden pheasant
    tail

Originator: Roderick
Haig-Brown, Vancouver
Island, B.C.
The Silver Brown first
appeared in Roderick
Haig-Brown's, *The Western Angler* (1939). This is a fly that has to be tried to be appreciated
because it really looks like a cutthroat or salmon fly when it is wet. Fished on a 12-foot
leader with a floating line, the Silver Brown is as deadly a low-water, autumn pattern as anyone could ask for on Olympic Peninsula or Vancouver Island streams.

Sea-run Cutthroat

Beach Fly
Hooks: #2-4, SALT
Thread: Black 3/0
Body: Silver Diamond Braid
Wing: Hot orange and yellow hair
Topping: Orange Krystal Flash
Head: Black tying thread

Originator: Randy Frisvold, Federal Way, Wash.
This easily tied fly is very effective when beach fishing in the fall for mature coho approaching spawning estuaries and rivers. It is also excellent for sea-run cutthroat trout. It is definitely a favored fly for Puget Sound waters.

Allard Fly
Hooks: #2-4, SALT
Thread: Black 3/0
Tail: Grizzly hackle fibers
Rib: Silver tinsel, fine
Body: Yellow chenille
Throat: Soft grizzly
Wing: White hair and orange flash

Originator: Al Allard, Tacoma, Wash.
This rediscovered Puget Sound pattern was developed in the 1960s for mature coho and sea-run cutthroats. It is fished along beaches for fish migrating towards their spawning rivers. The long, sparse wing provides lots of action on the retrieve. The K-Special Orange, a similar fly with an orange body, is also a top sea-run cutthroat pattern.

Cutthroat Candy
Hook: #8, Dry Fly
Thread: Tan Monocord
Overlay and Wing: Brown deer hair
Hackle: Brown, palmered
Body: Thin brown wool

Originator: Steve Raymond, Seattle, Wash.
Raymond has been using this fly, fished dry, for sea-run cutthroat in Puget Sound and Hood Canal with good success for nearly 20 years. Usually fish it the same way you would a traveling sedge, by skating it over the surface, although cutthroat will occasionally take it on a dead float. Other body colors may be substituted, and a clipped deer hair body will float longer.

Fly-fishing for Shad

*A*merican shad were stocked in California's Sacramento River in 1871 and in the Northwest's Columbia River in 1890 and now provide sport fishing in numerous coastal streams that enter the Pacific Ocean. Shad fishing can offer an exciting alternative to the vanishing runs of salmon and steelhead.

Shad are the largest species of herring, with an average length of 16 inches. They are hard-hitting fish that often clear the water in spectacular leaps, and are truly deserving of their nickname of the "poor man's steelhead." Best of all, they readily take flies. A growing number of anglers, including fly fishers, are becoming hooked on shad fishing as they discover the fighting ability of this fish.

Shad are anadromous, living most of their lives in the ocean, returning to freshwater rivers only to spawn. Two- to four-pound males begin entering coastal streams for their spawning run in late spring, when water temperatures climb into the 40s and 50s. Peak movement on the Columbia River occurs when the river is between 62 and 66 degrees. Males are soon followed by 4- to 6-pound females.

By mid-May large numbers of shad can be found in the Sacramento and Columbia river systems as well as numerous other coastal streams. The run continues for approximately four weeks before tapering off.

Shad don't feed once they enter fresh water, but strike flies in defense of their spawning grounds or just out of curiosity. Fish can be taken from boats, but wading streams to discover their migration routes provides an even greater sport.

Shad lay their eggs by broadcasting them on the surface. While the female is extruding 50,000 to 500,000 eggs, the male swims alongside to fertilize the eggs, frequently bumping her. It is a frantic process that takes place at night.

Shad

Fertilized eggs sink to the bottom and hatch in about six days and the fry remain in the river all summer. In the autumn, the 3- to 5-inch shad group and drift down to the ocean where they remain schooled for the next four to six years.

Locating Shad

As shad travel upstream, they congregate in narrow slots. Finding the slots might require covering the water systematically, as steelhead fishermen do, until all areas have been searched. Look for funnel water that forces fish into a narrow area. They sneak around the edges of fast water, eddy lines, and seams. They also seek depressions or other resting areas amid fast water. Look for nervous water, indicating it is running over an uneven bottom. Like steelhead, shad rest in deep pools above and below fast water. They might also congregate below bridge abutments. Look for water that is moving at a comfortable walking speed. Don't waste time on slack water.

Shad turn off and on to various colors; if they stop biting, try a different pattern. Shad also travel in waves so you might have to wait for a wave to arrive.

The best time to catch shad is early in the morning. They might stop striking in the middle of the day on bright days, and they don't take flies after dark because they become too absorbed in spawning activity.

Fishing Tactics

Whether fishing from the bank or a boat, the best place to cast is over water that's between four and 10 feet deep. Depth is critical since shad are usually on the bottom. A floating line with a long leader and a heavily weighted fly will work for slower shallow water. For fast water a fast-sink or sink-tip line with a short leader is required to get the fly down. The leader on a sinking line should be no longer than six feet, quickly tapered to 3X. Shad are usually not leader shy.

Cast downstream at a 35 to 45 degree angle, pause and let the line sink for a few seconds, then start a slow retrieve of one-foot strips. Give the rod tip an occasional twitch. Most shad are caught on a fly swinging across and down. Allow the fly to hang in the current or better yet in a seam next to the current at the end of each drift because shad will often strike the fly as it dodges back and forth. Casting a heavily weighted fly upstream and jigging it along the bottom on a downstream drift might be effective also.

There is nothing subtle about the grab. Shad don't have teeth, and a strike is like a short rubbery bump. When you feel the bump, set the hook, but avoid a strong jerk because shad have paper thin mouths. They are fierce fighters, and after a couple of runs it gets down to a tug of war. Play them quickly if you intend to release, but don't horse a shad or the hook will tear loose.

Tackle

Conventional trout rods that handle 5- to 9-weight lines are adequate if they have enough backbone to land a 5- to 7-pound fish rapidly. A nine-foot graphite is recommended. The reel should hold at least 100 feet of backing and have a good drag.

Weight-forward lines are best. Some recommend a floating line and a long leader, but sinking or sink-tip lines with short leaders make casting a heavy fly easier. Stout leaders (3X and 4X) will save time and tackle because heavy flies tend to snag the bottom frequently. Twist-on weight also can be used to increase sink rate. A long handled net is required for landing fish on rivers with rocky banks such as the Columbia.

Flies

Most Western flies for shad call for a short-shank hook and bead chain or dumbbell eyes one-third back from the eye. Dumbbell eyes also add the needed weight. A No. 6 hook is standard but carry a few No. 8s and No. 4s.

A basic pattern might consist of white or bright green calf tail beard that extends just below the hook point and a bright-colored body. Hot red, pink, chartreuse, fluorescent lime, white and yellow are also very popular as are colorful plastic chenilles. Flashy materials such as Krystal Flash or Flashabou should be used sparingly because too much flash might spook the fish. Bonefish flies often are effective.

Where and When to Fish

In Northern California, the shad planted in the Sacramento River a century ago now produce sizable runs in the Feather, Yuba, American, Klamath, Russian, and Eel rivers from mid-May to about July 1.

In the Columbia, shad fishing is excellent below and above Bonneville Dam, and it can be good near other Columbia River dams. The number of shad climbing the fish ladders at Bonneville and other Columbia and Snake river dams has been increasing quickly since 1959. Shad arrive at Bonneville by mid-June and at Ice Harbor Dam on the Snake River by early July.

In Oregon, Columbia River shad run up the Willamette River where they stack up below Oregon City Falls. Shad have spread down Oregon's coast to the Siuslaw, Umpqua, Coquille, and Coos rivers. The Siuslaw and Umpqua rivers have famous fly-fishing areas.

Shad Patterns

Pound Puppy Red
Hooks: #6-8, STLHD
Thread: Red nylon 4/0
Tail: Pearl Flashabou
Body: Red mono over silver tinsel
Wing: Pearl Flashabou
Hackle: White
Eyes: Dumbbell, with red pupils

Originator: Bill Schiffman, Gleneden Beach, Ore.
In *Shad Fishing*, author C. Boyd Pfeiffer states that most productive shad patterns are "simple, relatively big, cheap, and easy to tie and generally pretty gaudy." This pattern is one of the more gaudy flies. Bead chain or non-lead dumbbell eyes may be added for weight. A few strands of red Krystal Flash may be added to the tail.

Shewey Shad Shafter
Hooks: #4-6, Wet Fly, 3XL
Thread: Chartreuse 3/0
Tail: Marabou
Eyes: Non-lead dumbbell
Head: Chartreuse plastic chenille

Originator: John Shewey, Bend, Ore.
This is one of several shad patterns developed by Shewey for fishing shad runs from the Columbia River to Northern California. The tail is tied

in at mid-shank and extends beyond the hook shank. When tying the tail of this pattern, Krystal Flash may be added sparingly. Too much reflectiveness seems to scare—not attract—shad.

Shad

Red Devil
Hooks: #4-6, SALT, long
Thread: Red 3/0
Tail: Red Krystal Flash
Eyes: Dumbbell
Body: Red monofilament
Collar: Red Krystal
   Flash

Originator: John Shewey, Bend, Ore. Another attractive shad pattern published in

Northwest Fly Fishing: Trout & Beyond by John Shewey. Dumbbell eyes provide the weight required to help keep the flies close to the bottom. Light, medium and heavily weighted flies are needed for different water depths and current speeds.

Safety and Etiquette

A few things need to be considered when fly-fishing. They include caution and proper respect which make fly-fishing much more pleasurable.

Safety

Always fish with a buddy, and let people know where you are going and when you will return.

Fly-fishing can provide many hours of pleasure and excitement, exploring beautiful settings for sparkling, hard-fighting fish. But with these pleasures some significant potential dangers exist, including hypothermia, difficult wading conditions, and hazardous boating.

The water conditions that steelhead and salmon anglers encounter can be especially dangerous. The water is cold and the bottom can be slippery.

When winter fishing, wear layered clothing incorporating wicking, fast-drying synthetics to stay dry and warm. For wading safety, use traction devices on your feet, such as good felt soles or stream cleats. A wading staff is almost always prudent. A belt around the wader waist can be cheap insurance, and CO_2 inflatable suspenders or an inflatable vest can be a true lifesaver. When boating, consider safety always, use life jackets, and more importantly, use the right boat for the job, and use it safely.

Float tubers should wear personal floatation devices. The tubes in float tubes should be checked annually and the bladder replaced if there is any sign of cracking or wear from the covering. Entering and leaving the water with float tube and fins is tricky. If you don't have assistance, make each step very carefully. Be aware of approaching bad weather. Stay within swimming or kicking distance of shore. Keep your center of gravity low and use the

Safety and Etiquette

quick release on your seat to further lower your center of gravity if winds kick up high waves.

Wading, boating, and tubing fly fishers should take along a dry bag of spare clothing in case they get dunked. A fall into cold water can end a day's fishing unless a fly fisher has a change of clothing. Cold water or a strong wind can quickly cool the body to a hypothermic condition.

Etiquette

Etiquette is most important on popular and sometimes crowded waters. Fly anglers are generally a congenial bunch, but an otherwise fine day can be spoiled by bad manners.

When fishing in moving waters, unless you're the only one around, move steadily through a drift, taking a step or two after every few casts. Do not enter the water in front of another angler working through a run unless invited to do so. Instead, start a respectful distance away and follow the angler through. Consider using a different technique or fly when following another fly fisher. Many times a fish will pass up a first offering to take something different later. An angler who stays in one spot is usually not taking full advantage of all available water. It is permissible to fish to within a comfortable distance, leave the water, and then re-enter a cast or two beyond the stationary angler.

When you see a wading angler below you while you're in a boat, move to the other side of the stream if you can. Also, don't cast into a wading angler's water as you pass. If you can't avoid a wading angler, stop and ask which passage would be preferred. Generally, if you pass behind the angler, you won't disturb any fish. Communication between floating and wading anglers is the best way to avoid problems.

In stillwaters, overcrowding in a particular area can result in hard feelings unless anglers accommodate others' needs for space. Don't encroach on another angler's water by drifting or casting into it. Backward-moving float tubers and boat rowers need to look where they're going so they don't get too close to other anglers. Be aware of other anglers who might be in your back-cast area.

Fly anglers traveling in a power boat need to stay well away from other anglers—and slow down—as they pass or approach a fishing area.

If possible, inquire about and observe local rules of etiquette, and treat other fly fishers as you would want to be treated.

Catch and Release

*T*he Inland Empire Fly Fishing Club actively promotes catch-and-release fishing, and agrees with Lee Wulff's belief that a fish is too valued a creature to catch only once. The catch-and-release concept is becoming more important to fly fishers as greater numbers of anglers improve their skills at catching fish. To obtain the maximum benefit from our available resources, each of us needs to make our best effort to release fish unharmed. Fly fishers can use many techniques to reduce fish mortality.

First, use equipment sturdy enough to subdue the largest fish you might hook on a given trip. Following the fish's initial runs, play it relentlessly to bring it in as quickly as possible. Toward the end of a fight, the rod should be kept low, maintaining steady side pressure on a big fish.

Second, keep the fish from jumping against any hard objects, and don't drag it on shore to unhook it.

Third, if possible, keep the fish in the water while you unhook it with forceps or another release tool. Barbless hooks make this job easier. If necessary, use a wetted, soft-mesh net to control the fish. Avoid touching the fish if you can, but turning a fish upside down in the water will calm it.

Fourth, if resuscitation is necessary, wet your hands first, then gently hold the fish upright so it faces into a gentle current. In still water, move the fish forward by moving your tube or boat. When recovered, the fish will swim away on its own.

As for photography, some excellent pictures can be taken of fish in the water about to be released. If you must have an "air" picture of your trophy tell the photographer to focus just above the water, then pick up the fish and hold it at that point. Support it with both

Catch and Release

hands but don't squeeze it or touch its gills. Take the picture *quickly*, and put the fish back into the water.

In a Canadian laboratory study, researchers found that holding an exhausted fish out of the water even for a few seconds increased the chance that it would die. With 30 seconds of air exposure, 37 percent of fish died within 12 hours, and with 60 seconds air exposure, 72 percent died.

A hooked fish that burrows into a weed bed can't open and close its mouth to breathe. Usually a fish that dives into the weeds escapes within a couple of seconds. If it remains tangled, release the line tension or break the tippet allowing the fish to free itself. Keeping tension on the line and moving to the fish to untangle it increases the chances that the fish might die.

When water temperatures reach 65 to 70 degrees, many fly anglers quit fishing or move to the cooler high country. Warm water holds less oxygen and that stresses cold-water species such as trout. Adding the stress of being caught can be fatal to a fish. Daytime water temperatures of 65 degrees tell us that we should fish in the early morning or late evening when the water is cooler. At 70 degrees, quit fishing and wait for cooler weather or a rainstorm to cool the water.

Hooks

*T*here has been a revolution in fly hook manufacturing since the end of World War II. Early on, fly tiers depended on only a few brands to fill their needs. Among the best known were Mustad, of Norway, Partridge and Sealey of Great Britain, and Viellard-Migeon of France.

The Japanese realized that they would have to produce high quality hooks to compete with European hooks and it wasn't long before Tiemco, Daiichi, and Dai-Riki became familiar names to fly tiers.

U.S. and European manufacturers met this Japanese competition with new and improved hooks. Now, most manufacturers use high quality carbon steel and many hooks are chemically sharpened. With all the new processes, words like laser sharp, flashpointing, mini barb, micro barb, needle point, knife-edge point and others have entered the vocabulary of the demanding fly tiers and fly anglers.

The new high quality hooks are more expensive than the standard varieties still used by many tiers. Although tiers sometimes complain about the cost, they understand that the hook is the most important part of a fly pattern, and they buy, sometimes reluctantly, the expensive new-technology hooks.

Hook Specifications

We have made hook specifications by indicating only the differences, if any, from a "standard" hook. For our purposes a "standard" hook has a round bend, straight shank and turned-down eye.

Departures from the "standard" are indicated by an X with a leading number and a

Hooks

following letter. The number indicates the magnitude of the departure and the letter indicates the type of departure. For example 3XL means that a hook has the shank length of a hook three sizes larger, and 3XF means the wire diameter is equal to the wire in a hook three sizes smaller. So, our generic specification for grasshoppers and other long-bodied dry flies is #6-12, Dry Fly, 2XL.

The description in words is: Dry fly hook in sizes 6 to 12, with a 2 extra long shank. Several features of the hook are implied: "straight shank, round bend, and turned-down tapered eye," all of which are parts of a standard hook. Any hook, by any manufacturer, meeting these specifications will work just fine for grasshopper patterns.

The following abbreviations are used in this book:

L = Longer shank	TD = Turned down eye	RB = Round bend
S = Shorter shank	TU = Turned up eye	SB = Sproat bend
F = Fine diameter	SE = Straight eye	LB = Limerick bend
H = Heavy diameter		SC = Scud bend
W = Wider gap		CS = Continuous bend

DRY FLY HOOKS

SPECIFICATION	DAIICHI	DAI-RIKI	GAMAKATSU
Regular (1XW/SE)	1170/1180/1190	305/310	P10/S10S/S10U
1XF			
1XF,1XW (SE)	1100/1110		
1XF, SE (TU,CS)			S12S-1F/S135-M
1XL		300*	
1XS, 1XF, (SE/TU)	1310/1330		
2XL, 2XF (1XF, SE)	1280		
2XS, 1XF (SE,TU)	1480/1640		
3XF (4XF/1XW)			

NYMPH AND STREAMER FLY HOOKS

1XH, 1XW (2-3XH/SE)			L10-2H/S14S-3H
2Xl (1XW)			
2XL, 1XH (2XH)	1710	730	P10-2L1H
3XL (1XH/2XH)	1720	710	
3-5XL, 1-2XH, Bent Shank	1730	700B	C11-5L2H
3XL, SE, CS (1XH)	1270/1273	270	
4XL (1XH)	2220	700	
4XL, SE (1-3XH)	1750		S11S-4L2H
6XL, 1XH (LB)	2340		
DRAPER			
LB, 1/2 in. Longer (LE/SE)			
SB (1-2XH)	1550	075	S10/S10-B
SB, 1XL, 2XH (1XH)	1560	060	
SB, 3XL (4XL)			

SCUD HOOKS

SCUD, 1XF	1130		
SCUD	J220		C12
SCUD, 1-2XH (TU)	1150	135	
Egg			

STEELHEAD HOOKS

STLHD (General use)	2050/2161		T10-6H
	2441/2421		
STLHD, 1XF (Waking Patterns)			T10-3H

SALTWATER HOOKS

KEEL			
SALT (General Use)	2546	930	02410/SL11-3H
SALT, Long			

We have not specified barbless hooks, but we believe only barbless hooks should be used. Some hook models are manufactured barbless. Others can be made barbless by squeezing the barb with smooth-jaw pliers or squeezing it in the vise. We recommend doing this before you tie the fly because occasionally a point will break during the "debarbing" process.

Most tiers use regular or fine wire for dry-fly patterns and regular or heavy wire for wet flies, nymphs, and streamers. If you don't have the exact hook, use something close. Many tiers successfully use "dry-fly" hooks for wet-fly patterns and lighter "wet fly" hooks for dry-fly patterns.

The following tables provide a general relationship for hooks. Any hook models meeting the general hook specifications will be satisfactory. Comparable hook models are frequently not exactly equal.

DRY FLY HOOKS

MUSTAD	ORVIS	PARTRIDGE	TIEMCO
80000BR	JA4864/JA4641	L2A/L3A	
94840/94845	JA1523/JA1877		5210
			100/101/900BL
94859/94842		L3B	
7957B			
94838			501
94831	JA1639		2312/5212
	JA170T		921/500U
94833		E1A/E4A	5230

NYMPH AND STREAMER FLY HOOKS

MUSTAD	ORVIS	PARTRIDGE	TIEMCO
			9300
9671/AC9671	JA1524	H1A	
			5262
9672/AC9672	JA1526		5263
8100BR			
80050BR/80060BR	JA1510	K12ST/GRS12ST	200R
79580	JA8808	D4A	
9674/9674B	JA0167	D3ST	9395
	JA1511		300
		H3ST	
3665A/9575/36620		CS17	
3399/3906/3906B		G3A	3769
			3761
38941/33960			

SCUD HOOKS

MUSTAD	ORVIS	PARTRIDGE	TIEMCO
	JA1639		2487
37160/80250BR		K4A	205BL
80200BR	JA8891		2457
9174			

STEELHEAD HOOKS

MUSTAD	ORVIS	PARTRIDGE	TIEMCO
36890/80500BL	JA1645	Bartleet/N/M	7999
4049/90240	JA1644	O1/CS42	7989

SALTWATER HOOKS

MUSTAD	ORVIS	PARTRIDGE	TIEMCO
79666S			
3407/34007	JA9034	Sea Prince/Sea Lord	811S
34011		Sea Streamer	

Caddisfly Hatch Chart

Common Name (Genus species)	Hook Size	Larva: Cased or Free	Emerger: Wing Color/Body Color
American Grannom (Brachycentrus occ.)	10-18	Square Dark Case	Brown/Bright Green
Little Sister Sedge (Cheumatopsyche)	14-20	Olive Brown Larva	Brown/Bright Green
Little Western Weedy-water Sedge (Amiocentrus aspilus)	14-20*	Dark Case	Brown/Bright Green
Little Tan Short-horned Sedge (Glossosoma)	14-18	Pink Larva	Tan/Pale Green
Great Gray Spotted Sedge (Arctopsyche)	6-10*	Olive Brown Larva	Gray/Green
Spotted Sedge (Hydropsyche)	8-16*	Olive Brown Larva	Brown/Yellow
Green Sedge (Rhyacophila bifila)	10-18	Bright Green Larva	Brown/Bright Green
Brown Sedge (Lepidostoma)	14-18*	Square Dark Case	Brown/Brown
Speckled Sedge (Helicopsyche)	16-20	Not Applicable	Brown/Yellow
Late Grannom (Brachycentrus amer.)	12-16	Dark Case	Brown/Bright Green
Black Dancing Sedge (Mystacides)	14-18**	Slim Light Case	Black/Black
October Caddis (Dicosmoecus)	2-8	Yellow Larva or Medium Case	Brown/Orange
Mottled Sedge (Neophylax)	8-14	Light Case	Brown/Yellow

*Cased or free larva two to four hook sizes larger

**Cased larva hook size 4-10

Caddisfly Hatch Chart

Adult Body Color	Time of Emergence	J	F	M	A	M	J	J	A	S	O	N	D
Olive/Brown/Green	Morning/Mid-afternoon					▓	▓						
Pale Olive Brown/ Pale Ginger	Morning/Evening						▓	▓					
Greenish Brown	Evening						▓	▓					
Greenish	Sporadic						▓						
Pale Olive Brown/ Green/Dark Brown	Daytime						▓						
Tan/Brownish Tan/ Ginger	Morning/Evening							▓	▓				
Green	Evening							▓	▓	▓			
Brown Shades	Daytime							▓	▓				
Light Brown/ Straw Yellow	Evening							▓	▓	▓			
Olive/Brown/ Green	Early Morning								▓	▓			
Pale Yellow/ Black Wing	Morning							▓	▓				
Burnt Orange	Late Afternoon Until Dark									▓	▓		
Brownish Yellow	Late Afternoon										▓		

References

Almy, Gerald, 1978, *Tying and Fishing Terrestrials*, Stackpole Books, Harrisburg, Penn.

Arbona, Fred L. Jr., 1980, *Mayflies, the Angler and the Trout*, Winchester Press, Tulsa, Okla.

Bates, Joseph D. Jr., 1979, *Streamers and Bucktails: The Big Fish Flies*, Alfred A. Knopf, Inc., New York, New York.

Borger, Gary A., 1980, *Naturals: A Guide to Food Organisms of the Trout,* Stackpole Books, Harrison, Penn.

Borger, Gary A., 1991, *Designing Trout Flies*, Tomorrow River Press, Wausau, Wisc.

Combs, Trey, 1991, *Steelhead Fly Fishing: Tackle and Techniques, The Great Rivers, The Anglers and Their Fly Patterns*, Lyons & Burford, New York, New York.

Cordes, Ron and Randall Kaufmann, *Lake Fishing With a Fly*, Frank Amato Publications, Inc., Portland, Ore.

Crawford, Jim, *Salmon To a Fly*, Frank Amato Publications, Inc., Portland, Ore.

Curcione, Nick, 1994, *The Orvis Guide to Saltwater Flyfishing*, Lyons & Burford, New York, New York.

Cutter, Ralph, 1996, "California's Shad," *Western FlyFishing*, June, Frank Amato Publications, Inc., Portland Ore.

Davy, Alf, ed., 1985, *The Gilly: A Flyfisher's Guide to British Columbia*, Published by Alf Davy, Kelowna, B.C., Canada.

Dick, Lenox, 1996, *Experience the World of Shad Fishing,* Frank Amato Publications, Inc., Portland, Ore.

Federation of Fly Fishers, 1996, *Patterns of the Masters*, Vol. 5, The Oregon Council, FFF, Eugene, Ore.

Federation of Fly Fishers, 1995, *Patterns of the Masters, 30th Anniversary Edition*, The Oregon Council, FFF, Eugene, Ore.

References

Ferguson, Bruce, Les Johnson, Pat Trotter, 1985, *Fly Fishing for Pacific Salmon*, Frank Amato Publications, Inc., Portland, Ore.

Hafele, Rick and Dave Hughes, 1981, *The Complete Book of Western Hatches*, Frank Amato Publications, Inc., Portland, Ore.

Hafele, Rick and Scott Roederer, 1987, *Aquatic Insects and Their Imitations, For All North America*, Johnson Publishing Co., Boulder, Colo.

Haig-Brown, Roderick, 1939, *The Western Angler*, William Morrow and Company, New York, New York. [2nd Ed., 1991, Derrydale Press, Lyon, Mass.]

Hanley, Ken, 1994, *Surf Zone*

Herzog, Bill, 1994, *Guide To Lake and Stream Trout Fishing*, Frank Amato Publications, Inc., Portland, Ore.

Hughes, Dave, 1987, *Handbook of Hatches*, Stackpole Books, Harrisburg, Penn.

Johnson, Les, 1988, *How to Fish for Sea-Run Cutthroat Trout*, Frank Amato Publications, Inc., Portland, Ore.

Juracek, John and Craig Mathews, *Fishing Yellowstone Hatches*, Blue Ribbon Flies, West Yellowstone, Mont.

Kaufmann, Randall, 1991, *Tying Dry Flies*, Western Fisherman's Press, Portland, Ore.

LaFontaine, Gary, 1981, *Caddisflies*, Lyons & Burford, New York, New York.

Ligas, Kenn M., 1992, *The Fly-Fisher's Manual*, Bozeman, Mont.

Mandell, Mark, and Les Johnson, 1995, *Tube Flies: A Tying, Fishing & Historical Guide,* Frank Amato Publications, Inc., Portland, Ore

Martin, Darrel, 1994, *Micropatterns*, Lyons & Burford, New York, New York.

McCafferty, W. Patrick, 1981, *Aquatic Entomology*, Jones and Bartlett Publishers, Boston, Mass.

McMillan, Bill, 1987, *Dry Line Steelhead Fishing*, Frank Amato Publications, Inc., Portland, Ore.

Meyer, Deke, 1992, *Advanced Fly Fishing for Steelhead*, Frank Amato Publications, Inc., Portland, Ore.

Nemes, Sylvester, 1975, *The Soft-Hackle Fly*, Chatham Press, Old Greenwich, Conn.

Nemes, Sylvester, 1981, *The Soft-Hackle Fly Addict*, by the author, Chicago, Ill.

Nemes, Sylvester, 1991, *Soft-Hackled Fly Imitations*, by the author, Bozeman, Mont.

Pfeiffer, C. Boyd, 1975, *Shad Fishing*, Crown Publishers, Inc., New York, New York.

Pfeiffer, C. Boyd, 1995, Shad Flies, "Simplicity with a Pedigree," *American Angler*, May-June, Abenaki Publisher, Inc., Bennington, Ver.

Raymond, Steve, 1994, *Kamloops: An Angler's Study of the Kamloops Trout*, Frank Amato Publications, Inc., Portland, Ore.

Richards, Carl, Doug Swisher and Fred Arbona Jr., 1980, *Stoneflies*, Winchester Press, New York, New York.

Shaw, Jack, *Fly Fish the Trout Lakes,* Mitchell Press, Ltd., Canada.

Shewey, John, 1992, *Northwest Fly Fishing: Trout and Beyond*, Frank Amato Publications, Inc., Portland, Ore.

Solomon, Larry and Eric Leiser, 1977, *The Caddis and the Angler*, Stackpole Books, Harrisburg, Penn.

Steeves, Harrison R. II and Ed Koch, 1994, *Terrestrials*, Stackpole Books, Harrisburg, Penn.

Taylor, Marv, 1994, *Marv Taylor's Float-Tubing the West*, Belly Boat Publishing, Boise, Ida.

Thornton, Barry, 1994, *Saltwater Fly-fishing for Pacific Salmon*, Hancock House, Blaine, Wash.

Usinger, Robert L., Ed., 1956, *Aquatic Insects of California*, University of California Press, Berkeley, Calif.

Originators of Variations, Individuals Popularizing Patterns, and Fly Tiers

Ackerlund, Bill
Aigner, Boyd
Allard, Al
Balek, Walt
Baller, Jeff
Balser, Eric
Bates, Bob
Beatty, Al
Bibbee, Loyd
Biggs, George
Borden, Bob
Borger, Gary
Britton, Les
Britton, G. L.
Brown, Ron
Burk, Ed
Butler, Glen
Carlson, Don
Caryl, Everett
Chan, Brian
Chinn, Don
Clarke, L. J. Graham
Cook, George
Cooper, Del
Coppock, Del
Crawford, Jim
Cubley, Walt
Cunningham, Al
Darling, Tom
Deaver, Alice
Drain, Wes
Dritz, Harry
Eagle, Wally
Evans, Dennis
Faggetter, Harry
Ferguson, Bruce
Findlay, Clay
Foreman, Dan
Frisvold, Randy
Gaddy, Jim
Gahlke, Jake
Gidlow, Arnie
Goddard, John

Good, Bob
Griffith, George
Gunderson, Dave
Haig-Brown, Roderick
Halladay, Leonard
Harms, Jerry
Harrop, Rene'
Haufler, Carl
Henderson, Bruce
Henry, Cliff
Hoffman, Henry
Hogan, Dec
Holmes, Dave
Jackson, Alec
Jansen, Frans
Johnson, Les
Jones, John
Juracek, John
Kaufmann, Randall
Kembietz, Joe
Kennedy, Mike
Knapp, Frank E. Jr.
Knudson, Al
LaFontaine, Gary
Langenhorst, Hubert
Lawson, Mike
Lemaich, Dan
Lemire, Harry
Ligas, Kenn
Lorenson, Gene
Lynch, Gene
Martinez, Felix
Mathews, Craig
Matson, Boyd
Mayo, Harry
McBride, Jerry
McLeod, George
McLeod, Ken
Mikulak, Arthur "Mitch"
Newbury, John
Noble, Mark
Norton, Howard
Olson, Gordon

Pelzl, Bob
Perry, John
Pinch, Mark
Prankard, Dick
Propp, John
Quigley, Bob
Raymond, Steve
Richards, Don
Richards, Carl
Roope, Joe
Ross, Irv
Roth, Phil
Runje, Mike
Sadlo, Jan
Schiess, Bill
Schiffman, Bill
Shaber, Randy
Shaw, Jack
Shearer, Jim
Shewey, John
Shiosaki, Fred
Slak, Frank
Smith, Brett
Smith, Elmer L.
Smith, Charles
Stranahan, Chuck
Sullivan, Virgil
Swisher, Doug
Thompson, Richard B.
Tollett, Tim
Troth, Al
Trotter, Pat
Turck, Guy
Upton, Charles
Waller, Lani
Ward, Ed
Williams, Taylor "Beartracks"
Wolen, Ben
Wolfe, Ed
Wright, Phil
Zug, Cliff

Fly Pattern Index

Notes

Notes